# David Leach

David Leach finishing the neck on a large bottle, 1976.
*Photograph courtesy of John Anderson.*

# David Leach

A Biography by Emmanuel Cooper


## David Leach – 20th Century Ceramics

Exhibition Catalogue by Kathy Niblett

RICHARD DENNIS
2003

# Acknowledgements

Many people have helped in the preparation of the book, but I must thank, above all, David and Elizabeth Leach, who have not only answered numerous questions, searched for references and photographs but offered warm hospitality far beyond the call of duty. I would also like to thank David's sister Jessamine Kendall and his sons John, Jeremy and Simon. Others I would particularly like to mention are Tim Andrews, *Ceramic Review* archive, Crafts Study Centre, The Surrey Institute of Art and Design, University College, Farnham, David Horbury, Kathy Niblett, Bob and Mary Rogers, Oliver Watson and David Whiting.

EC

The exhibition and book to celebrate the life and work of David Leach have been made possible by the consistent support of many people.

It has been a pleasure to work with David Leach and to be made so welcome into his home by Elizabeth, his wife of 65 years. John Leach and Tim Andrews have put me right on technical matters when the historian's view 'got in the way'; thank you both.

The initiative for this celebration came from John Leach in conjunction with The Devon Guild of Craftsmen. I am pleased to acknowledge very warmly the administrative work undertaken by Alexander Murdin, Director and Jenny Plackett, Assistant Director of The Guild. They have been towers of strength in raising funds and making the exhibition a reality.

We are grateful for grant-in-aid provided by The Arts Council of England's National Touring Programme, which has made the tour possible.

Lenders have been very generous in agreeing to be parted from their pots for many months. I extend many thanks to individual collectors from whom the majority of pots has been borrowed. Without their support neither the book nor the exhibition could have happened. David's collectors, his supporters over many years, prefer to remain anonymous but my thanks are no less heartfelt. I am grateful that museums and collections have also lent significant pots:

Pamela Wood, The Castle Museum, Nottingham - Ballantyne Collection; Miranda Goodby and Susan Taylor, The Potteries Museum & Art Gallery, Stoke-on-Trent – Dr Henry Bergen Collection; Richard Green, York City Art Gallery - The Milner-White Collection; Angie St John Palmer, High Cross House, Dartington Hall, Devon – Dartington Hall Trust Collection; David Grant, Highland Stoneware Limited, Lochinver, Scotland; Leah and Philip Evans, The Round House Gallery, Foston, Derbyshire; The Rudolf Strasser Collection, Munich; Tim Andrews; Richard Batterham; John Leach; Elizabeth Raeburn.

I have enjoyed co-operating with Emmanuel Cooper, who has written an excellent and well-deserved biography of David Leach. Wendy Wort at Richard Dennis Publications has successfully co-ordinated the widely scattered contributors to the book in her usual efficient and pleasant way.

Lastly, I must thank my greatest supporter of all, my husband Paul.

KN

Photography of ceramics by Magnus Dennis

Print, design and reproduction by Flaydemouse, Yeovil, Somerset

Production by Wendy Wort

Published by Richard Dennis, The Old Chapel, Shepton Beauchamp, Somerset TA19 OLE, England

© 2003 Richard Dennis, Emmanuel Cooper, Kathy Niblett

ISBN 0 903685 89 2 softback edition, ISBN 0 903685 88 4 hardback edition

British Library Cataloguing-in-Publication Data. A catalogue record for this book is available from the British Library

# Contents

| | | Page |
|---|---|---|
| Preface  *by David Whiting* | | 6 |
| Foreword  *by Oliver Watson* | | 8 |
| Introduction  *by Emmanuel Cooper* | | 9 |
| Chapter One | The Early Years, Japan, China, England, 1911-1930 | 11 |
| Chapter Two | The Leach Pottery, St Ives, 1930-1945 | 19 |
| Chapter Three | Consolidation and Innovation, David Leach at St Ives, 1945-1955 | 27 |
| Chapter Four | 'The Craftsman's Way of Life', South Devon, 1955- | 38 |
| Chapter Five | Elegance and Strength – The Individual Pots | 50 |
| Chapter Six | National and International Success | 57 |
| David Leach – 20th Century Ceramics  *by Kathy Niblett* | | 71 |
| Backstamps | | 112 |
| Chronology | | 113 |
| Principal Exhibitions | | 114 |
| Public Collections in the United Kingdom and Overseas | | 116 |
| Articles, Books and Films | | 117 |
| Assistants, Apprentices and Students at Lowerdown Pottery | | 119 |

David Leach, first pot, Abiko, 1917.

# Preface
# David Leach – The Eye of the Heart

On the back of an exhibition invitation David Leach sent to me in the early nineties, he wrote: "Just to let you know that I am still at it in a senile sort of way! Innovative creativity on the decline, but always trying to improve on past experience". Such remarks are typical of David – typical of a self-effacement, honesty and self-deprecating humour which has lived hand-in-hand with the deepest artistic convictions. However, they also reveal that persistently youthful outlook – an outlook continually eager to learn and delighted by the daily revelations that pottery brings him. A distinctly patrician and dapper façade (there is a certain grandeur about this potter) soon falls away as he becomes engaged in conversation, fixing you with those unflinching but twinkling eyes as he absorbs the latest news of exhibitions and craft world manoeuvres – his interrogations punctuated by animated responses and often loud bursts of infectious laughter.

That he remains such a vivid and vital personality is another aspect of that essential youthfulness. He has always seized the moment. Still very palpable is the young boy who was so amazed by the broad Japanese landscape that he surveyed from a high tree with his father way back in 1918. Still there is the boy we all know from Bernard's touching and lyrical portrait etching – the lad in the photograph so absorbed by Mr Pascoe's jug making at Truro Pottery in 1923 (page 17). There persists in him an air of innocence, of questioning self-doubt, along with the certainty and dedication. It is this exacting tension that has fed and driven the particular spirit of his work, a continuing quest into all the ramifications of form, glaze and decoration. Anyone who has closely studied a David Leach exhibition will see how that process of augmentation and refinement continues. Alongside the graceful porcelain and majestic dolomite and temmoku stonewares, there will be quite new and often unexpected integrations. Even in his nineties, when most potters of his age would have settled into a stylistic routine, he has the ability to surprise. David may be almost as old as the studio movement, but it is difficult to think of anybody as concerned with the *status quo*, even if it does not always meet with his approval. As he once wrote so eloquently of our now obligatory personality cult; "How consciously egocentric our art and, I fear, our craft have become in this century; we have all become like Narcissus, ever looking in the mirror at our shrinking images".

David remains extraordinarily generous with his time and advice, particularly where the young are concerned. Well known is the public service in crafts education and administration, but the people he has helped on an individual basis are countless. David is a great listener, quite one of the most interested men I know. And if he is philosophically 'Leachian', his father's son, he is far more catholic in his cultural tastes than one might assume. I always think his great sense of fun is part of the theatre of the man, the contemplative potter who has also proved such a fine and entertaining artistic ambassador, lecturing and demonstrating all over the world – the man who might well, had things been different, become an actor.

David is firm (some might say stubborn) in his aesthetic beliefs, but this has not prevented him from being a great pragmatist – following a very practical and empirical course that has produced some of the most beautiful and resolved designs in modern ceramics, a body of work as informed by the science of pottery as his intuitive insight. When he once spoke of his friend Harry Davis as being "as much an engineer as he was a potter" he might well have been talking of himself. This relates not only to his professional absorption of ceramic processes, but more broadly, to the organisational skills and foresight that made the Leach Pottery a viable concern. And then we must consider the functional balance and operation of his tablewares. Long before the emergence of the so-called 'New White' in the nineties, David was producing some of the most economic and quietly conceived celadon porcelain in the discipline. There is a subtle precision about this work, but also a developed appreciation of a pot's innate motion as well as stillness. We find in that now famous fluting not only restraint but the discernable quiver, the slight tremor of the maker's eye and hand – a quality that gives these objects all the synergy and life of artistic experience. They also have a quintessential modernity. As the critic Bill Ismay wrote of Leach's appreciation of history; "His cut flutings on pots of essentially twentieth-century feel are among the most sensitive done by anyone since the technique was classically developed by Oriental potters".

The sight of so many pots assembled together in this book is a moving and sobering experience. Here is the manifest proof of workshop continuity, a discipline of rhythm not just in the making but in the living. David's intimate awareness of the fabric of pottery is revealed in the fluency of his forms, in the indescribable spark of his carving and engraving, in the resist willow patterns on big dishes and jars and the calligraphic swipes down opulently glazed bottles. David once talked about the importance of "a performance in work where the inventive heart and mind are conveyed very quickly into what the hand can do, with very little interruption between the mind, heart and hand". When he stressed that you can only add to such a tradition of making, the Leachian tradition, through personal expression, he made it clear that those who merely imitate have not understood the 'fullest intent' of this credo. Meanwhile, looking at the shapes, surfaces and colours here that David has made his own, it is clear that his art has all the authority and resonance of a singular vision, of a gaze that penetrates deeply. To see how his pots can shape and enliven a room is to understand how this craft can get under your skin; a craft which in David's hands truly has what the artist Cecil Collins called "the eye of the heart".

David Whiting
November 2002

# Foreword

David Leach is one of the great unsung heroes of British studio pottery. Well, perhaps not entirely unsung, but surely not sung loudly enough, or often enough. A modest man, averse to self-promotion, he has not enjoyed (if that is the word) the regular magazine profiles, monographs and retrospective touring shows that have adorned the careers of his peers, and indeed of younger generations, many of his students, and now even of their students. Like his father, Leach is blessed with a long, active life. His father – now there's the rub.

David's role in relation to his father's work has been the making of him (and indeed the making of his father), but has also formed a carapace – a structure difficult for him to shed, and difficult for us to see clearly through.

Without the Leach name and connection, his achievements would be notable. He was the first to bring to the craft workshop both technical know-how and managerial competence, skills in both design and in marketing. He realised the needs of a production pottery which could operate efficiently without compromising deeply felt ideals in making, in art and in life. And he has taught this to the craft world in the most impressive way – by living and making according to these standards for some seven decades.

The context in which he has achieved this makes the work more impressive. He saw his father struggling and failing, not in his ideals but in their realisation. He saw his role was to provide the technical and managerial support, without which Bernard Leach would have gone bankrupt, and perhaps ended merely as a footnote to, rather than the prime mover of, the British studio pottery movement. David was clever and courageous enough to see that he must seek help from the 'enemy', the industrial devils of Stoke-on-Trent. He persuaded his father's backers to back him, in the teeth of his father's wishes, and he returned and demonstrated his worth by ensuring the continuation of the St Ives Pottery. This feat was the prelude to the development of St Ives standard ware, which in its style, methods of making, marketing and selling has been perhaps the single most important and influential type of English studio pottery ever made. Bernard may have had the prime artistic vision (most of it anyway), but without David it would never have seen the light of day. But David's achievement here is hidden beneath the carapace of the epic Leach story (the Bernard Leach story, that is).

This would be enough to earn David a place among the heroes. But his later achievements are as impressive though, this time through his own modesty, equally hidden: his rigorous training of students, both at St Ives and later at Bovey Tracey, his involvement in teaching and in the establishment of other potteries, his development of a specialist hard-paste porcelain, suitable for studio use. And above all, his pots. Like the man, unassuming and unpretentious, and like the man, steadfast in their integrity, quality, and generosity. To fill a life as a potter making pots such as these is a remarkable achievement. To have played such a crucial part in the most important and formative story in British studio pottery is a remarkable achievement. To realise how different the studio pottery story in this country would have been without him, makes him a remarkable man and potter. It is in tribute and in grateful recognition of both man and potter that this book and retrospective exhibition have been produced – a reminder to us all and those who follow of what it takes to be a hero.

Oliver Watson
Victoria and Albert Museum, London, November 2002

# Introduction

During a lifetime devoted to pottery, David Leach has made, and continues to make, a unique contribution to contemporary studio ceramics, both as a sensitive and gifted potter and as an educator seeking to encourage a deep understanding of the processes of the craft. As the son of the world famous potter Bernard Leach, he started work in his father's Pottery at St Ives primarily with a view to being a member of a team rather than as an individual artist potter. For twenty-five years he was his father's right-hand man, efficiently and effectively running a team of some dozen potters. He introduced wide-ranging technical innovations, devised better and more effective ways of working, and collaborated with his father on designing a range of new tableware. Occasionally he made his own individual pots but he saw his main responsibility as manager rather than artist, primarily enabling his father to produce his own work. It was only in 1955 when he decided to set up his own workshop, Lowerdown Pottery at Bovey Tracey, that David's gifts as a creative potter were fully realised.

At Bovey Tracey he produced earthenware for five years before making high-fired wares. At the same time he began to produce individual pieces in stoneware and porcelain alongside the range of tableware. Quiet, unassuming, contemplative forms were where his interest lay, and he has pursued such concerns ever since. Honing, refining and developing his skills and understanding of his chosen materials, he continues to produce distinctive and sensitive pots. Like his father, David Leach has been concerned with appreciating an oriental aesthetic through European understanding. Forms are often those produced in the great classic periods of Chinese art, such as the Song Dynasty, and the colours are those of the earth – soft creams and beiges, grey-blues, dark browns and blacks, and muted greeny greys. Decoration is abstracted from flowers, plants and landscape, though none attempts to represent it in any direct way. The primary concern is that of form itself, with decoration being used to enhance it.

Since his birth in Tokyo in 1911, David Leach has been aware of two cultures – East and West – and recalls the family home as an English home within a Japanese house. In Japan he was trilingual, speaking Japanese, some Chinese after the family spent time in China, as well as English. When the Leach family came to England in 1920 and settled in St Ives, he was a regular visitor to his father's Pottery, occasionally giving a hand but with his eyes set on a career in medicine rather than the arts. As he gradually came to recognise that his father was 'about something', it seemed to him that he 'could be useful' in the Pottery doing all those practical things that his father did not do so well.

So began a career as a potter that has spanned over seventy years. In that time he has produced a consistently well-designed and made range of tableware as well as highly distinctive individual pots, exhibiting widely both in this country and abroad.

Alongside his work as a potter, David has been involved in education, first and most notably at Loughborough College of Art and later on the Harrow Studio Pottery Course, and he has also been a visitor and an examiner at many other schools of art. In the 1970s he played a pivotal role in setting up the Dartington Pottery Training Workshop, giving advice and support to an organisation in which trainees could learn the craft from professionals. David Leach has also been instrumental in promoting wider understanding of studio pottery, supporting the Craftsmen Potters Association of Great Britain, a co-operative organisation that set up a successful shop and gallery and serving as a focus for studio potters for the exchange of news, views and information among their and its supporters and the pioneering work of the Devon Guild of Craftsmen.

As critics, commentators and cultural historians continue to redefine the paradigms of craft, and observe the blurring boundaries between craft, design and technology, referencing this to visual mainstream practice, it is timely to make a full assessment of the contribution of David Leach. Making pots for him involves the whole of the mind and the body; it requires a scattering of philosophy, great skill, practical ability, business understanding and a working knowledge of science informed by an artistic sensibility. Being a potter, he thinks, is a rounded, highly satisfying existence. In his nineties David Leach is still making pots, continuing to relish the challenge of resolving technical and artistic problems and still eagerly awaiting the opening of the kiln after a firing. This book tells the story of this extraordinary man and details his many achievements, but it is his pots that will stand as a testament to his rare creative abilities.

EC

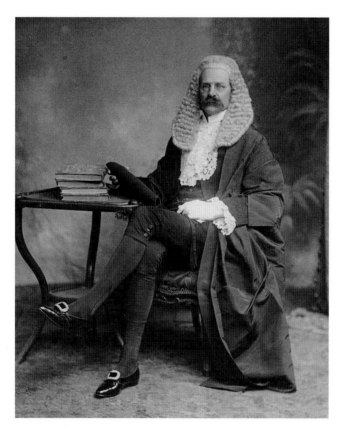

Andrew John Leach (David's grandfather),
judge, Penang, Singapore, c.1885.

# Chapter One
# The Early Years, Japan, China, England, 1911-1930

David Leach as a baby with his father and mother, Tokyo, 1913.
*This photograph was given by Bernard Leach to Alan Caiger-Smith's grandfather.*

David Leach in centre with his mother and brother Michael on left, and sister Eleanor on right, Tokyo, 1917.

David Leach was born in Tokyo in 1911, the eldest of five children – two boys and three girls – to Bernard and Muriel Leach. His father, the only son of a colonial judge, is generally acknowledged as one of the founders and leaders of the studio pottery movement and as a major figure within the twentieth century visual arts world; he is also widely recognised both for his work as an artist potter and as a spokesman on the importance of ceramics as an art form able to stand alongside painting and sculpture. His mother, Muriel Hoyle, was also an only child. Her father was a doctor and scientist, Director of the Manchester Museum and later Director of the National Museum of Wales; her mother was a keen supporter of literature and the arts. Through his parents and from his childhood in Japan, China, and St Ives David gained a unique introduction into both the life of an artist and first-hand experience of widely differing cultures, all of which informed his understanding of ceramics and his own work.

## Family background

David's father, Bernard Leach, was born in the East and educated in the West. In Japan he learnt the craft of potting, and throughout his life saw himself as a courier between the two cultures. After studying drawing and painting in London in 1909 he travelled to Japan, inspired partly by the pioneering spirit of his ancestors and partly by the romantic writing on Japan by Lafcadio Hearn. He had intended to teach etching, a technique that hitherto had been little practised in the country, and also to marry his cousin Muriel. Before she arrived he had a traditional, single-storey wooden Japanese house built on Ueno Hill, consisting of two twelve-foot square rooms, two smaller rooms, kitchen and bathroom and most importantly a fair-sized studio. The building, a blend of traditional Japanese and Western style, symbolised the family's hopes for life in Japan. Here David's parents settled with two servants to live in reasonable comfort.

The Leach family at Carbis Bay, St Ives, left to right, Eleanor, Jessamine, David, Michael, Muriel, Bernard, Betty, Mary Streuli, 1923.

## Childhood

The weeks leading up to the birth of the Leach's first child in 1911 were an anxious time for both parents-to-be as they recalled the tragic death of Bernard Leach's mother who had died while giving birth to him. However, all appeared to be going well and when Muriel announced that the birth had started there seemed no cause for anxiety, although it proved to be for them both the beginning of a twenty-four hour ordeal. In the evening Muriel was put to bed and, after a restless night, the baby was born on the morning of 7 May 1911. 'Never will I forget the first cry of the babe, and the first sight of him. I feared for a few minutes he was dead, but soon he made it clear that he was not', noted his father in his diary, adding 'Poor little chap, he's not so handsome. About 8lbs with a big head and fairly fat.'[1] The infant thrived, weighting a robust 10lbs 12ozs at six weeks and was named David Andrew.

Two years later, on 12 May 1913, David's brother, named William Michael, was born. Family life quickly settled into a familiar routine, and as the children grew older there were regular readings aloud of such classics as Keats's poems *Ode on a Grecian Vase,* and *Nightingale*, which their father thought 'amazing', and other popular classics that included *Marie Clare* by Marguerite Alldoux, *Simon the Jester* by William John Locke and Thomas Hardy's *Jude the Obscure,* Kate Douglas Wiggin's *Rebecca of Sunnybrook Farm*, Rudyard Kipling's *The Jungle Book* and R. D. Blackmore's celebrated historical adventure *Lorna Doone.*

Like many other European families, in the hot sticky summer months the Leach's escaped to the cooler mountain air. Favourite spots were the picturesque and unspoilt mountains and lakes of Hakone, about a hundred miles from Tokyo, the result of volcanic action that culminated in the beautiful Mount Fuji, and the mountain resort of Karuizawa, about a hundred miles north of Tokyo, near the active Asama volcano. It was here, during their last

Bernard Leach, 'Sleep in the Hills, My son David', 1918. Drawing, ink and wash, a simplified representation of landscape that Leach was to follow throughout his life. Signed BL. h.252mm. w.312mm. The Board of the Trustees of the Victoria and Albert Museum, London.

visit in 1918 that David, then seven years old, fearlessly climbed the tallest tree with his father, fully fifty feet above the ground, to look out over miles of grassy planes fringed by mountains. For one summer holiday the family rented a thatched cottage by Lake Hakone, a magnificent stretch of water six miles long and one-and-a-half wide renowned for its shimmering reflection of Fuji. To help care for David, 'not a crying child', they took with them 'nice, responsible maids', which allowed Bernard and Muriel the freedom to explore the countryside and enjoy invigorating walks, climb hills and row on the lake. Such idyllic spots were 'lovely places to dream and draw', and during these holidays Bernard Leach did most of his work on paper. One drawing features his eldest son lying on a hillside apparently asleep.

At a raku party Bernard Leach was introduced to the art of pottery, and was so smitten by the process that he studied for two years with Urano Shigekichi, a traditional potter working in a court style who held the title the Sixth Kenzan, the title by which Leach referred to him. With Kenzan Leach learnt how to throw on a Japanese wheel, to fire a raku kiln and gain experience of firing to high temperature.

## China

At this time, despite much interest in various art forms, including pottery, Bernard Leach did not define himself as a potter and was generally uncertain about his direction in life. He felt dissatisfied with his career in Japan and, in search of some central purpose in his life, came under the influence of Dr Alfred Westharp, a Prussian Jew who had embarked on a mission to 'save China' from Western influence. Leach wanted to collaborate with Westharp and despite Muriel being seven months pregnant with their third child, decided that he and his family should settle in Peking. On 4 July 1915 they duly embarked on board the *N Y K Keiko Maru*, arriving in Peking after an appalling voyage feeling tired and disorientated but ready to settle in the country.

In China the Leach household, consisting of two cooks, an amah with tiny bound feet to look after the children, a house coolie, a donkey coolie and a water carrier, established itself independently on Westharp's country property just outside the capital. It was not a promising outlook. None of the staff could speak English nor could the Leach's speak Mandarin, and communication was possible only through gestures and the use of a phrase book. In addition the family found the heat intolerable, while the hoards of mosquitoes added to their discomfort, forcing them to sleep under a secure net; the farm next door attracted swarms of flies, which were a continual irritation. Despite this the children adjusted reasonably well though their health was not good. David was dosed with invalid food to improve his blood, while Michael often suffered from painful stomach cramps. Westharp, who regarded himself as an authority on education, advised Bernard and Muriel to put the children in a separate building some distance away, advice that under the circumstances seemed unnecessarily cruel and which Muriel dismissed as an 'unnatural arrangement'. Meanwhile David had made friends with the local Chinese children, whom Muriel thought 'working class' and 'smelly', but conceded were also 'natural ' and 'healthy'.

With the imminent birth of Muriel's third child, the family moved to Peking, settling in a house not far from the wall round the old city, where the baby, named Edith Eleanor was born. The children, in particular David, were soon integrated into the neighbourhood, making friends with, among others, Jung Hai, one of the coolies. With Jung, David explored the ancient city wall, which though not vast seemed very large to the small child. In the courtyard David, often wearing an elastic band round his head to stop his ears sticking out, pushed Michael about in a chair on wheels, and played with the local children and as a consequence soon learnt to speak fluent Mandarin. Leach's relationship with Westharp, however, was breaking down and he abandoned the idea of 'saving' China, and late in 1916 returned with the family to Japan with a plan to establish his first pottery.

## Tokyo and Abiko

In Tokyo the Leach family settled in the residential and commercial suburb of Aoyama, in Harajuku, a few hundred yards from the tramways and not far from English and American friends. Their traditional-style house was raised from the ground and had a porch, a veranda, windows fitted with paper shutters rather than panes of glass, and was of sufficient size to accommodate the immediate family, a maid and a cook. The large sitting room had communicating sliding doors that led into the dining room, and tatami matting covered the floors. David, then a child of six,

Bernard Leach, etching, David Leach, 1920. David was born in 1911 in Tokyo. Signed BL on plate. h.159mm, w.148mm. Crafts Study Centre

remembers it as having an upstairs though he slept downstairs as did the maid who helped to look after the children. The house had a garden and a separate tearoom where his father slept. In the absence of suitable Western-style furniture Bernard Leach created his own, designing tables, a bookcase, chairs and a settee that were built by a local carpenter. It was, remembers David, an English home set within a Japanese house. Many of the meals were English and included such favourites as porridge, rice pudding and custard.

At the invitation of Soetsu Yanagi, an influential Japanese critic and writer, Bernard Leach set up his pottery studio in Abiko on Yanagi's estate, twenty-five miles from Tokyo, leaving Muriel to manage the home and care for their three young children. Although initially favouring the Montessori educational system that had been advocated so strongly by Westharp, in the absence of specialist opportunities David was dispatched to a local kindergarten, along with Japanese children. Here he sang songs and quickly added fluent Japanese to his English and Chinese. A year or so later he was sent to an American grammar school at Skiji to study with other European children, travelling alone occasionally by fixed-wheel bicycle. The journey, which involved crossing the city and passing the Imperial Palace with its gardens and moat was quite an adventure for a young child, but his biggest fear was not so much the distance but the possibility of getting his bicycle wheels caught in the tramlines. In the evening as the children went to sleep their parents often sang them the traditional Japanese lullaby 'Nen nen Yo' (Mother carried you on her back, Mother cradles you in her arms, Good babies do not cry.). On the whole the children, though boisterous, were well behaved, but in a letter to her husband from the holiday mountain resort of Karuizawa, Muriel indicated her anxieties and frustrations. 'I can't get any peace' and the children irritate me so dreadfully though I can't say they're naughty. Eleanor is the difficulty, I've nothing for her to do, the boys would be no trouble otherwise'.[2]

During a visit by Muriel and the children to Abiko in the spring of 1917 they experienced at first hand the power of Oriental thought when David was painfully stung by a hornet. The village carpenter, Sako, who was building the studio, reassured him that it could be cured, and taking the child on his knee told him to be still and repeated the words of a *sutra*, a Buddhist sacred text, and with one finger wrote its Chinese characters in the air. 'Now', he said 'it's alright', and much to everyone's amazement, it was.[3]

## England

With the children growing up and Europe more settled following the ending of the war, Bernard and Muriel decided to return home to allow their children to have an English education, and for Leach to set up a pottery in St Ives, Cornwall. A cabin was booked for the family on the *N Y K Kamo Maru* leaving Yokohama for London in June 1920, with a single berth for Hamada, a young Japanese potter who admired Bernard Leach's pots and who wanted the experience of working in the West.

During the long voyage the family got to know Hamada, who proved to be affable and friendly with a gentle sense of humour, and a great success with the children. Endlessly patient, he spent time playing with them on deck, teaching David to swim in a makeshift canvas swimming pool by urging him to doggy paddle from one side to the other. His involvement was gratefully received by Muriel who was seven months pregnant, and shortly after arriving in Britain she gave birth to twins, named Ruth Jessamine, known as Jessamine and Elizabeth Massey, known as Betty.

Frances Horne, a philanthropist who lived in Carbis Bay, a mile-and-a-half from the town, sponsored the Pottery in St Ives; she had set up an organisation known as the St Ives Handicraft Guild that employed local women to produce a variety of weaving and embroidery, and saw a pottery as a useful addition to the Guild's activities.

Bernard Leach packing the kiln, assisted by David Leach, shortly after the kiln had been built, St Ives, c.1925.

## St Ives

In September 1920 Leach and Hamada settled in St Ives at number six Draycott Terrace, a handsome late-Victorian terrace house built originally for sea captains, which overlooked Porthminster Beach, the harbour, Godrevy lighthouse and the railway station. They were soon joined by Muriel, the children and a Swedish *au pair*. The house proved rather cramped and a year later they moved to number fourteen, which was a little larger. The boys were dispatched to a small local school run by Miss Shakerly, popularly known as Ma Shaps, and when David reached the age of eleven he was sent to a preparatory school in Clifton, Bristol, though David cannot now recall how or why this school was chosen.

In 1922 the family moved yet again when Bernard Leach bought an old granite building, Providence Count House[4], set back a hundred yards from the main road in Carbis Bay. Then divided into two, it was turned into one large house, the dry rot treated and a gable added to the long sloping roof to provide four extra rooms to the ten that already existed. The roots of a eucalyptus tree planted by Havelock Ellis, a previous tenant, which threatened to disturb the walls, was also dealt with, though the family were convinced that the reek of eucalyptus kept them free of colds. The light and airy upstairs drawing room had windows looking across the bay to Godrevy Lighthouse, while a huge, well-worn Chinese carpet with a faded design of blue dragons, two large blue-and-white dishes hanging on the wall and Oriental pots standing on shelves added to the slightly exotic atmosphere. A red hand-woven Ethel Mairet blanket was draped across the back of the sofa. The furniture was a combination of traditional but comfortable English pieces with one or two from the East. The one drawback was that the house tended to be damp and the family waged a more or less continual battle with cockroaches, usually hitting them with a shoe.

Hamada continued to spend hours talking and playing games with the children. One hot summer day he and Bernard had a wager that David and Michael could not swim the distance round the headland from Porthminster Beach to Carbis Bay. From a rowing boat they watched as the boys floundered in the water, Michael giving up about three-quarters of the way, David just managing it. Both were rewarded with a half-crown (12.5p) for their efforts. On one memorable occasion the whole family attended the opening of an exhibition of their father's pots at the Paterson Gallery, Bond Street, celebrating afterwards with a meal in the *Shanghai*, one of the few Chinese restaurants in Soho, which David recalls as notable for orders, in full, quarter or half portions, being shouted down the dumb waiter to the kitchen below.

At the age of thirteen David (and later Michael) was sent to Dauntsey's School, Wiltshire, a non-denominational institution established over 400 years earlier by William Dauntsey. Catering chiefly for the sons of farmers, Dauntsey's was less expensive than many schools, and David remained there until 1930. Much to his father's relief, Michael won a school scholarship to Cambridge University, which meant a reduction of a third in the fees. Like his father David excelled in sports and drama rather at the expense of academic subjects, and often had to make several attempts to pass examinations. As a keen sportsman David went on to become a county hockey player and captain of Cornwall. He played rugger for the St Ives Rugby Club as well as a tennis and cricket club player.

During the school holidays David initially showed little interest in the activities of his father's Pottery, unlike Michael who was fascinated by watching the throwers, and for a School Speech Day constructed a small kiln and made pots. Eleanor and Jessamine were sent to Badminton School and both later trained in dance. Betty who suffered from cerebral palsy, then known as spastic paralysis, remained at home and was in many ways the centre of Muriel's life.

As the children grew, the pattern of family life was largely determined by school holidays during which their father took them for walks and played games. Family outings involved long cliff top walks and, in good weather, picnics, when a fire was built to boil the kettle. There were visits to old mines to scour for Fools Gold or quartz crystals and long summer rambles gathering wild strawberries. In the autumn they collected blackberries and made jam. A great treat was trailing black treacle over Cornish cream spread on 'splits', the name for a Cornish roll, which his father thought resembled the appearance of the way in which lines of different coloured slip decoration flowed into each other.

Mr Pascoe, Michael Leach, Hamada, Bernard Leach and David Leach watching how to attach a pulled handle to a pot, c.1921.

Indoors they played Racing Demon, Up Jenkins and Head, Body and Legs. In the garden they enjoyed French cricket while in the nearby Tregenna rhododendron woods there was the hide and seek game of Sardines. In the evenings their father, often lying on his stomach, read aloud classics such as *The Rime of the Ancient Mariner* by Samuel Taylor Coleridge. Occasionally the family gathered round the gramophone to listen to Harold Samuel play Bach or the *Double Violin Concerto in D Minor* as well as Paul Robeson singing Negro spirituals, but a recording of a Japanese *No* play invariably reduced the children to uncontrollable giggles. There was also the pleasure of watching their father play cricket for Lelant Cricket Club, and admiring his skill as both a batsman and bowler. In many ways it was an idyllic childhood.

On one occasion the family, together with Hamada, made a trip to Truro Pottery, a long-established traditional Pottery to see how they worked. David, his father and Hamada watched fascinated as one of the potters, Mr Pascoe, pulled handles on the side of a jug, a technique that was new to them. A photograph records the event, with David, a lad of about eleven, wearing a large Boy Scout hat. Although not at that time intending to make his career as a potter, it was such events, and the evident skills the work involved, which were to make a deep impression, and to play a part in David's decision to take up the craft.

**FOOTNOTES**

1. Bernard Leach, *A Potter's Book*, London, Faber and Faber, London, 1940.
2. Muriel Leach letter to Bernard Leach, 1917. Leach archives 344, Crafts Study Centre, Surrey Institute of Art & Design, University College, Farnham.
3. Bernard Leach, *Beyond East and West*. London, Faber and Faber, London, 1978, p.117.
4. The house had belonged to the long defunct Providence Tin Mine.

## Chapter Two
# The Leach Pottery, St Ives, 1930-1945

Shortly after his nineteenth birthday David Leach, much to his father's surprise, asked to join the Pottery. David had initially thought he might follow in the footsteps of his mother's father, Dr William Evans Hoyle, and study medicine, but as he later recalled, 'I was not clever enough to get a scholarship to university and my father was an impecunious artist who couldn't possibly afford to send me there without one.'[1] Although while at school he had not seen himself taking up the craft, he had started to spend more time watching the potters at work and was beginning to realise that his father was 'about something which was unique and potentially universal'. Despite doubts about the Pottery's financial survival and with income rarely exceeding expenditure, his father was overjoyed to welcome a member of the family into the St Ives team.

In 1930 the Leach Pottery was going through a difficult period. Not only was the general economic situation depressed, but the sales of both his father's individual stoneware and porcelain pots and the tableware failed to meet the costs of running the workshop. With no overall plan to ensure the efficient running of the Pottery, Bernard Leach was continually looking for ways of raising funds. In addition to poor sales, the general lack of technical understanding led to many mishaps, with stoneware bodies developing disfiguring bumps, known as bloating, during the firing while the earthenware was often too porous and unhygienic for use as tableware; the pots also had a tendency to chip.

David Leach carrying a board of pots, mostly domestic tableware, Leach Pottery, St Ives, 1932.

19

David Leach throwing, Leach Pottery, St Ives, 1939.

There were also problems with retaining a skilled work force. Few of the steady stream of students who came to work at the Pottery in search of practical experience stayed after they became proficient, preferring to set up their own studios. In an attempt to increase sales and ease the financial situation, the workshop was reorganised in the hope of producing a more regular range of well-fired tableware that could be sold relatively cheaply as 'bread and butter' lines. With a slightly more ordered programme of making tableware, one or two of the skilled throwers did remain at the Pottery.

## The Pottery

Built on the outskirts of St Ives, the Pottery was intended for a small team of potters, with areas for clay preparation, glazing, and throwing. Under Hamada's direction an Oriental-style, wood-fired climbing kiln for stoneware and porcelain was constructed, but this rapidly deteriorated and was rebuilt three years later by a professional Japanese kiln builder.[2] A round, up-draught kiln was constructed for earthenware and raku. As far as possible the Pottery sought to use Cornish clays and glaze materials, acquiring a local red clay for low temperature wares, but in the end had to compromise by bringing in ball clays from Devon to make up the stoneware body. The individual pots in stoneware and porcelain were made by, or under the direction of, Bernard Leach, as were individual large slip-decorated plates in the style of Toft and other seventeenth-century Staffordshire potters, which were also decorated by him. Assistants made the tableware in earthenware.

David Leach joined a small team. This included George Dunn, an ex-miner and fisherman, and possibly smuggler, who had helped build the Pottery and who stayed on as general help, preparing the clays, mixing glazes and such like. In addition there was Muriel Bell, a Canadian potter who stayed for three years. She was an excellent thrower and taught David basic pottery techniques. Charlotte Epton, who had arrived in 1927 and was later to marry the artist Edward Bawden, was also a competent thrower, able to pass on her skills to others. She left in 1931 following a dramatic fire when damp wood stacked on top of the kiln to dry caught alight in the early hours of the morning, burning down the roof as well as an adjacent store and in the process destroyed much of her own work.[3]

In 1931 Barbara Millard, 'a lovely South African girl', came to work at the Pottery, having studied at the Central School of Art, and stayed for a year, her good looks and vivacity making a great impression on David. Other able workers included John Coney who subsequently left to set up a pottery in Somerset and, briefly, Kenneth Murray between stints as an enlightened education officer and pottery advisor in Nigeria. Bernard Forrester arrived after having served a seven-year apprenticeship at Mintons in Stoke-on-Trent before studying at Armstrong College, Newcastle-on-Tyne where Herbert Read introduced him to the qualities of Song ware and suggested he contact the Leach Pottery to gain practical experience. In 1931 Laurie Cookes came to work at the Pottery, employed primarily to assist with the secretarial work and to look after the showroom, but having some potting experience she lent a hand at whatever tasks were required.

In 1932 Harry Davis, a highly energetic and technically skilled twenty-one year old potter, was taken on as a skilled worker. After studying at Bournemouth Art School, Davis had worked at Broadstone Pottery, Bournemouth where, learning from an old industrial thrower, he became a highly efficient. At Broadstone, which had produced giftware decorated with enamels or multi-toned 'dribbly glazes', Leach Pottery wares were discussed, not because of their aesthetic qualities but because they were able to command what seemed enviably high prices. When recession forced Broadstone to close, Bernard Leach offered Davis work at St Ives on a weekly wage of £1.10 shillings (150p). Davis's skills were greatly admired, and he not only threw the earthenware but also taught David professional throwing techniques.

David soon became aware of the lack of any overall organisation and the many technical failures at the Pottery, and saw that his possible contribution was to make the business more efficient. Like his father he was particularly horrified when during the high-temperature firings bungs of saggars fell over, ruining the work and many weeks of effort. He was equally appalled by the small number of first-class pots coming from the kiln, when bits of grit stuck to the surface marring their appearance, and by their tendency to develop splits at top temperature. Even the earthenware firings could be problematic. During one firing the back of a large slip-ware dish, decorated with a trailed design of a Japanese well, exploded, ruining many of the other pieces in the kiln. Although severely damaged at the back, the front survived more or less intact and was rescued by David.

Aware that his father was more of a thinker and designer than organiser and maker, David saw himself less as an individual potter and more as a member of the team, ready to acquire skills and deal with practical matters, and so fulfil that aspect of the business. It was a realistic assessment of need and, as he found, he learnt as much if not more from other people working at the Pottery than his father, who was not really involved in the making of the tableware. 'He designed rather than made production ware.'

## Dartington

By 1932 the financial situation had not improved and Bernard Leach saw a possible solution was to accept a long-standing invitation from Leonard and Dorothy Elmhirst to set up a pottery at Dartington in south Devon. In the mid 1920s the Elmhirsts, wealthy and philanthropic, had instigated an ambitious programme of rural regeneration, which included setting up a progressive school and a series of small craft-based industries as well as introducing radical farming methods on the old Dartington Hall estate. As great admirers of Bernard Leach's work and ideas, they were keen to have his involvement in the project and to establish a pottery workshop at Dartington Hall. While tempted by financial security and wealthy patronage, Leach had initially declined their overtures as he did not want to forfeit his artistic independence. In an attempt to allay Leach's fears, during a tour of Cornwall with Rabindranath Tagore, the Indian writer and advocate of social, educational and agricultural reform, they visited St Ives to further discuss Leach's involvement with Dartington. To the young David Leach, Tagore, with his long flowing beard, looked like the Old Testament prophet, Abraham, commanding awesome respect.

In addition to increasing financial problems, Bernard Leach had become emotionally involved with Laurie Cookes, and the move to Dartington was a useful escape from the emotional pressures of family responsibilities. In 1932 he settled in Dartington to investigate the possibility of setting up a pottery and also undertake a small amount of teaching, leaving David, who was still relatively inexperienced, to work with the St Ives team. Two years later Bernard Leach accepted an invitation from Yanagi and the National Craft Society of Japan to make an extended tour of the country, and David moved to Dartington to continue the experiments started by his father, leaving Harry Davis and Laurie Cookes at St Ives.

At Dartington, with a wide-ranging brief, David Leach fulfilled his father's teaching commitments, his students including the future MP and *bon viveur* Clement Freud, whilst continuing with research into setting up the new workshop. He built a slightly more efficient wood-fired kiln and investigated various raw materials, and also become better acquainted with the Elmhirsts. As the research continued he began to recognise the limits of his own technical knowledge, and how much he might benefit from a period of technical training in Stoke-on-Trent. Accordingly, in September 1934, leaving Bernard Forrester to take over his teaching at Dartington, funded by the Elmhirsts, he enrolled on the three-year Pottery Managers' Course at North Staffordshire Technical College. Although the course was geared exclusively to industrial manufacture, he saw the technology of clays, glazes and firing as of great relevance to studio potters. Less useful were the mechanised methods of production such as slip casting and jigger and jolleying, methods of mechanically making pots with the use of moulds.

Bernard Leach was appalled at his son's decision and dismayed that he had agreed to study in what he described as the 'land of the industrial devil', and that it would 'do him more harm than good'[4], believing that idea and concept should come before technical skill. As an alternative he proposed that his son spend a year in Japan to acquire a wider understanding of pottery, but no firm offer of help or funding was ever made. Recognising that a sound technical grounding would not be forthcoming from his father but that such knowledge was essential if the pottery at Dartington was to be set up on a secure foundation, David welcomed the opportunity to study ceramic technology, reasoning that aesthetic understanding would follow. 'Despite the fact that I was in a totally alien atmosphere learning the science of pottery on a Pottery Managers' Course, all industrially slanted and nothing to do with the world of the studio potter, nevertheless it was an opportunity to learn things one couldn't have learnt elsewhere...to do with fuels, firing, glaze behaviour and so on but I was perfectly clear as to what I wanted and I was prepared to toe the line as far as the course was concerned'.[5] Paradoxically, David Leach's technical knowledge was to become sufficiently advanced so that fifteen years later he found himself advising pottery material suppliers in Stoke itself, enabling them to offer materials to craft potters that would be useful to them.

Inspired by his brother's commitment to the Oxford Group, a revivalist Christian organisation set up in the 1920s by Frank Buchman[6] and which in the late 1930s took the name Moral Rearmament (MRA), David also became a follower. Michael Leach had been introduced to the movement while studying biological science at Cambridge University and had become deeply involved with it. With no temples, endowments, membership, subscription, badge, rules or definite location, the Group was made up of Christians who declared they had surrendered their lives to God, advocating the essential basis of all Christian faith as absolute honesty, purity, unselfishness and love. Accepting the belief that God can guide you, ideas were discussed at meetings known as House Parties and campaigns were planned to spread the word as part of Christian evangelism. After investigating the movement in Stoke-on-Trent, David accepted an invitation to a 'house party' conference in Harrogate. Here he was 'hit between the eyes' by the arguments and sense of commitment, returning with friends for the following weekends. With its emphasis on the importance of listening for God's direction on moral values and on putting faith into action, for David Leach the Oxford Group was 'the most effective way of focusing my Christian life'.

Although David Leach returned to the Pottery at St Ives during vacations, the workshop was largely run and organised by Harry Davis and Laurie Cookes who, after experiencing an initial lack of direction, felt that more business was required and taking matters into their own hands toured the country to acquire orders and dutifully produced the necessary pots. Davis, critical of the ware, made many technical improvements to both the clay body and the kiln, which resulted in stronger and more robust pots. As a result the Pottery began to operate more efficiently, even yielding a small profit, which, however modest, was a great improvement on previous years. However, with David Leach's course in Stoke coming to an end and him planning to return to St Ives, Davis decided to leave and eventually took a job in West Africa.

Bernard Leach returned from Japan with not only a wider knowledge of Japanese pottery but also a decision to end his marriage to Muriel and remain at Dartington where he and Laurie would live together. It was a great shock for all the family, and his father's decision presented David with something of a dilemma. Like Michael he continued to be involved with the Oxford Group and was supportive of his mother, but he also had some sympathy for his father for not only was he deeply committed to working with him, but had doubts about vows of monogamy. 'I was in my early twenties, I suppose I really didn't accept a monogamous view of marriage, and thought it natural for men to be susceptible to other women, and felt it in myself. But I also felt great sympathy for my mother, and anger that she had been hurt. My views were not consistent.'[7]

## Radical reform at St Ives

With his father now settled with Laurie in Dartington and spending much of his time writing his most important volume, *A Potter's Book*[8], David Leach returned to St Ives in 1937 planning to use his hard-earned knowledge in Stoke to reorganize the Pottery into a viable and sustainable business. During a visit to Dartington he had met and fallen in love with Mary Elizabeth Facey, known as Bubby, who was working as a physiotherapist. One of four children born to a retired naval surgeon living in Hayling Island, her mother, believing that in addition to her two sons her two daughters also needed a career, sent one to Lady Margaret Hall and Elizabeth to study at Guys Hospital in London. David and Elizabeth were married in 1938 and after carrying out considerable improvements designed by Peter Marr, a local architect, settled in Pottery Cottage. Their first child, John Henry, known as Johnnie, was born a year later, to be followed by Paul Jeremy in 1941. Although a decision had been made in principle to set up a new pottery at Dartington, the unsettled international situation with war looming on the horizon led to the idea being put on hold, though Bernard Leach continued to live at Dartington until 1941.

David's extensive programme of modernisation at St Ives was far-reaching, leading the Elmhirsts to conclude that it would be more useful to reinvigorate the Pottery than to set up a pottery at Dartington, and to all intents and purposes the idea was abandoned. Over a period of three years the Elmhirsts generously agreed to provide an annual sum of £1000 to cover salaries, running expenses and capital outlay. As a result the electricity supply was increased, a small amount of machinery was purchased to carry out mechanical tasks and a small electric kiln, made by the Applied Heat Company, with one cubic foot chamber, was acquired for tests. More dramatically, the large three-chamber kiln was converted from firing with wood to firing with oil. Wood was a scare commodity in Cornwall, and while Bernard Leach held the view that it was the only fuel able to achieve the sort of qualities he wanted in high-temperatures firing it was costly in terms of labour. David's proposal to modify the firebox to take oil burners and introduce wood only at the end to 'toast' the body was eventually accepted by his father. Although oil was used widely in industry, little was known about adapting it to fire a three-chamber studio pottery kiln and a certain amount of trial and error was required. As the blower had to be in continuous use firing with oil was noisy, and the process was also smelly but it speeded it up while yielding good results.

Most fundamentally, the actual production of pots was reorganized in a more professional way, for David saw that the Pottery could not go on making pots in a haphazard, sleepy fashion. Dicon Nance, with David's help, designed the Leach kick wheel, an efficient, three-legged, triangular-shaped, treadle-operated wheel with a heavy flywheel, built by a local carpentry firm. With the potter sitting as the wheel was kicked, this proved an excellent machine allowing the potter sensitive control, and became the preferred wheel for many potters.

For the Pottery to survive David saw that a skilled regular workforce was required, which was in great contrast to the steady stream of enthusiastic but unskilled students and trainee potters on which the Pottery had relied. Accordingly, he initiated a system of apprenticeships whereby school leavers were employed to be trained professionally, selected for their practical aptitude rather than artistic talent. The first two – William (Bill) Marshall and George Whittaker – were taken on in 1938, eager to learn about the preparation of clay and glazes, throwing and turning pots, and kiln packing and firing, all geared to serious production rather than leisure time or artistic activity. They were taught all pottery processes, including using weighted amounts of clay to throw pre-determined shapes to a measured size. Bill Marshall became a highly skilled potter and a mainstay at the Pottery, producing standard ware and, from the 1950s, his own pots, remaining until 1977. Over the years other apprentices were accepted for an initial three years and it proved to be an effective way of establishing a permanent and able team. Students still came to work at the Pottery, but it was less reliant on their day-to-day contribution.

David Leach also thought that a new range of tableware was required that should be made in the more robust and hardwearing stoneware. Under his father's direction he devised a range of pots for use on the table, in the kitchen or even in the oven, which were thrown to a measured shape and size from a known weight of clay and made in the tougher stoneware, so bringing the regular production of earthenware to an end. After his father had drawn the shapes David made prototypes, which were discussed and, when the final forms agreed, the dimensions, weight and shape of each pot were recorded as a guide for future reference. The extensive range included egg bakers, salt, pepper and mustard pots, beakers, casseroles, ash-trays, jam pots, tea and coffee sets, bowls, plates and jugs. With the outbreak of war, one of their salesmen recommended that they add a soup jug and bowls, with the idea that hot food could be served in air raid shelters.

These pots, sufficiently uniform to enable them to be ordered from a catalogue, became known as Leach Standard Ware and with modifications continued in production until Bernard Leach's death in 1979. The clay body was also adjusted to make it more workable and reliable as well as more attractive. Having learnt to appreciate the quality of unglazed clay from Japanese country potters, Bernard Leach agreed to David's suggestion that some pots were glazed only on the inside with either a creamy white, a pale green celadon or a deep black-brown temmoku, leaving the rich toasted body on the outside. This subtly contrasted the smoothness and colour of the glaze with the texture of the clay body.

Decoration was minimal, though some jam pots were painted with a flowing design, while those in porcelain often had an incised pattern of an oak leaf on the lid, beautifully shown off under a pale green glaze. Fruit or cereal bowls, thrown with a turned foot, were covered with a creamy-white glaze and decorated with three iron brush strokes in the form of a 'z', carried out by the team. The motif could be read as the Japanese character kò, meaning craft. Prices ranged from under a shilling (5p) for a small jug to fifteen shillings (75p) for a large. The general impression was of sound, practical design incorporating a feel for clay, the earthy, subdued colours suggesting wholeness and health with an appropriate degree of restraint.

Alongside the standard wares that now formed the bulk of production, Bernard Leach made individual pieces, which were fired in the large kiln. These were then sold under the name of the maker and the Pottery. Such a system became the model for many studio potters throughout the world, and continues to be accepted as a sound, workable basis for a small pottery, amalgamating art and skill, spanning the gallery and the craft shop.

The changes initiated by David Leach were effective. Though still tricky, firing the kiln by oil worked, shortening the firing time by 20-25% and yielding more reliable results. A new celadon glaze proved attractive, while a more efficient system for mixing the clay body was also successful. Making schedules for the throwers based both on fulfilling orders and the most economical way to fill the kiln, resulted in a steady stream of saleable pots, though initially orders had to be searched for. 'I went all over the country in a battered two-seater Morris with two suitcases of samples in the back: as far as Scotland, and jolly pleased with a £5 order on the books'[9], remembers David.

## War

The onset of war seriously disrupted production. Not only were controls introduced on raw materials, but also all members of the team, other than Bernard Leach, were eligible for military service. The ending of the Elmhirst funding in 1940 forced the Pottery to become self-sufficient, and to maintain viability, David, aware that new outlets for the pots were required, tenaciously approached shops in London. With all decorated industrially produced pottery shipped to America as part of the export drive there was a dearth of distinctive ceramics, and as a consequence useful orders were obtained from London department stores such as Liberty, Peter Jones and Heals, shops that hitherto would not consider taking their pots but were now keen to fill empty shelves. Sales at the Pottery for the quarter covering Christmas totalled £126.10s.9d (£126.55p), an improvement on the previous quarter and the same period a year earlier. Although modest, the sum was considered 'reasonable', and if maintained over twelve months would make the Pottery self-sufficient.

The reality of war was vividly brought home on 25 January 1941 when around nine in the evening a landmine was dropped on the Pottery by a stray German bomber. In its position above the town the Pottery served as an air-raid warden post, and on this particular night David was on duty. His father, who was temporarily staying at Providence Count House, heard the tremendous explosion and rushed outside to identify the cause. Over a poor telephone line David told his father that a half-ton bomb had landed in the vegetable garden blowing off the gable end of Pottery Cottage and severely damaging Penbeagle Cottage. The Pottery roof was also damaged but the supporting granite walls had withstood the blast. With Pottery Cottage rendered uninhabitable David,

Elizabeth and their son moved to Providence Count House, which was once again divided to enable them to have a separate establishment.

A temporary awning over the kiln enabled production to continue, and with two firings yielding some 2,500 pots, many of which were orders, Bernard Leach was convinced that they were 'well on the road to recovery'[10]. Conscription as well as enemy action restricted production as one by one the regular team were called up; Horatio Nelson Dunn, who worked as a general help preparing the clay body and packing pots, to the Royal Naval Reserve and Bill Marshall to be an army driver. But it was David's call-up in September 1941 that looked set to seriously affect the viability of the Pottery and caused Bernard Leach to leave Dartington and return to St Ives to manage the team and recruit new potters. Although inclined towards pacifism, he had even considered joining the Cotswold Bruderhof community[11], David failed to avail himself of the conscientious objectors tribunal and was ordered to report for duty to the Devon and Cornwall Light Infantry at Dorchester. After much protest and a spell of imprisonment, he rationalised that a Christian could also be a soldier, donned the uniform and spent the war in training recruits.[12]

A long letter to David written by his father towards the end of the war conveys the deep affection and respect each had for the other. His father, having left David's mother, attempted to set out the complexity of his feelings about Muriel, the importance of his relationship with Laurie (whom he had married in 1944), and his recently declared commitment to the Bahá'í faith.[13] The question of religious faith was one father and son regularly discussed, partly because of David's commitment to Moral Rearmament, which his father did not share, and because his father hoped to persuade David of the relevance of the Bahá'í faith and interest him in its activities. In fact David did attend meetings and enjoyed many aspects of the relaxed and informal assemblies, but decided that it offered nothing that was not already familiar in Christian belief.

It is a persuasive letter, not least because while acknowledging the close bond between a father and his eldest son, it also outlines the basis of their business relationship within the Pottery and his intention to make David a partner. It was the start of a highly productive ten years, in which David Leach not only consolidated his skills but also began to venture into wider areas, including education.

**FOOTNOTES**
1. Quoted in Mary Lean and Anastasia Stepanove, 'Good for a Thousand Years', *For a Change*, Vol. 14, no. 2, April/May 2001, page 6.
2. The three-chamber kiln, built by a 39th generation Japanese potter named Matsubayashi, was the first to be built in the West.
3. Early assistants included Michael Cardew, Katharine Pleydell-Bouverie and Norah Braden, all of whom went on to establish themselves as distinguished potters and interpret Bernard Leach's ideas in their own work.
4. Bernard Leach letter to the Elmhirsts, 24 August 1934. Leach Archive 5952, Crafts Study Centre, The Surrey Institute of Art & Design, University College, Farnham.
5. David Leach, Robert Fournier ed *David Leach: A Potter's Life, with workshop notes*, Fournier Pottery, Lacock, Wilts, second edition 1979, page 10.
6. An American Lutheran minister.
7. Interview with author, 29 May 1996.
8. Published in 1940 by Faber and Faber.
9. Fournier, page 12.
10. Bernard Leach letter to Muriel Rose, 29 May 1941. Leach archive 289 Crafts Study Centre, The Surrey Institute of Art & Design, University College, Farnham.
11. An international community movement rooted in Anabaptist and early Christian traditions, committed to non-violence, justice, and fellowship.
12. A reluctant recruit, he twice refused to wear military uniform and was hauled in front of a military commander who, having just returned from Dunkirk was full of fury for Nazi Germany, felt totally unsympathetic to David's pleas and sentenced him to 28 days detention. On his release the order to wear uniform was repeated and again refused, resulting in three months in military prison. With neither civilian clothes nor army uniform he eventually returned to the camp shrouded only in a blanket to the taunts of Gandhi.
13. The Bahá'í faith was started in the nineteenth century in Persia, and was an amalgam of Christian, Muslim and oriental beliefs, committed to equality and peace.

# Chapter Three
# Consolidation and Innovation
# David Leach at St Ives, 1945-1955

With the ending of the war in August 1945 David Leach returned to the Pottery as manager, a return that more than suited his father, for his son had proved to be a capable potter with a sound head for business. Having initiated radical change he efficiently handled the running of the workshop and the training and organisation of the workforce, which left his father free to pursue his writing and other activities. As confirmation of his trust in his son's abilities, David was made a partner the following year. With the restrictions on the control of materials slightly relaxed, David initiated further improvements; these included slightly extending the Pottery building, purchasing an electrical blunger for mixing the clay slip and an electric pugmill for preparing the plastic body. A little later an electric kiln suitable for biscuit firings was acquired. An indication of the Pottery's growing reputation was the increasing numbers of students wanting to work there.

With the Pottery now destined to remain at St Ives rather than move to Dartington, Bernard and Laurie, with their adopted son Maurice, moved into Pottery Cottage, while David continued to occupy one half at Providence Count House, with his mother and Betty in the other. At the Pottery the workers conscripted to the war slowly returned, and the old team was re-established. Like many other businesses, shortages and the need for permits, which continued in the early post-war years, affected trade, but sales of the standard ware remained buoyant. Between them the four or five throwers working at the three Leach kick-wheels averaged several thousand pots a year, and with most industrial wares continuing to be sent for export, regular bulk purchases for standard ware continued to be placed by large London department stores. Despite the imposition of purchase tax (to be replaced by VAT in 1973) on pots, which increased prices considerably, demand continued to rise, though the changes in levels of tax prevented up-to-date price lists being issued. In 1946, aware of the danger of relying on the London stores, David issued a mail order catalogue illustrating the standard wares. Yet, despite full order books and high demand, profits remained modest.

Under David Leach's able management the Pottery had, for the first time, what would later come to be known as a sound business plan. The working day began at eight and finished at five with a break in the morning, known as crib, an hour for lunch and a break for tea. Saturday was a half-day when visitors were welcome to see pots being made. Wages were modest and to supplement their income and foster their development as individual potters, throwers were encouraged to make one-off pots in their own time that could be sold in the showroom, the potter receiving a third of the selling price. A loose system of profit sharing was introduced to encourage and reward hard work. Two more local lads Kenneth Quick, nephew of Bill Marshall, and Joe Benny were taken on as apprentices. Kenneth Quick, slight of build, sharp and lively, proved to be an excellent and sensitive potter, keen to learn and develop his style. His fondness for practical jokes (on one occasion substituting the ice cream on a cornet with white clay) made him a likeable and popular member of the crew. Both Benny and Quick were called up for National Service in 1950 and a new apprentice Walter Firth accepted. The final apprentice, Scott Marshall, was taken on a year later at the age of fifteen. He eventually left with Richard Jenkins, a student at the Pottery, to set up the Boscean Pottery at St Just.

Bernard Leach, in the centre, in front of the corner fireplace in the Leach Pottery discussing the finer points of a jug with, from left to right, Frank Vibert, Mary Gibson Horrocks, Eileen Newton, from top right clockwise, Joe Benney, David Leach, Horatio Nelson Dunn, Kenneth Quick, Valerie Prescott (née Bond), 1947. Leach very much enjoyed these talks.

On his discharge from the army Michael Leach returned from Africa with his wife Myra and two-year-old daughter Alison, wanting to work at the Pottery. With little experience of production potting, both his brother and father were reluctant to take him on, believing him to be temperamentally and practically unsuitable for either the role of manager or worker, and suggested that he gain more experience. For a time he worked at the long-established Wreccelsham Pottery in Farnham before moving to Stoke-on-Trent and the studio of Bullers factory to assist the Danish-born potter Agnete Hoy in making individual pieces of porcelain. In the late 1940s he moved to St Ives and settled in Penbeagle Cottage, adjacent to the Pottery, and began to work at the Pottery, combining this with teaching at Penzance Art School, taking classes started by his father and David under the principal Edward Bouverie-Hoyton. When David and Bernard Leach were away Michael shared the management with Bill Marshall and Frank Vibert.

Students continued to come for longer or shorter periods. Among others these included two young American potters Warren and Alix MacKenzie in 1950, and with their help David virtually rebuilt the three-chamber kiln, which was by now in poor shape. This involved relaying the foundations, enlarging flues in the combustion chamber and using better refractories, but no change was made in the basic design. Firings took about twenty-four hours with wood being used for the final hour-and-a-half, primarily to create a wood ash, which was carried through the kiln to react with the exposed ware.[1]

Student training involved group discussions, particularly after a firing, when losses, failures and gains were considered. Bernard Leach's favourite theme for the discussion, 'What is a good pot?' was closely followed by David as debate touched on the choice of materials, the use of appropriate texture, colour and pattern and the balance of form as well as such details as the size of the foot, the thickness of the rim and shape of a handle. Some idea of the intimacy of such discussions is conveyed in a photograph taken shortly after the war in which Leach sits next to the fireplace in the Pottery surrounded by David and assistants. To mark the return to full production a large exhibition was held at William Ohly's Berkeley Galleries in Mayfair, London. Symbolically the exhibition was a restatement of the creative output of the Pottery, demonstrating its survival and its twenty-sixth anniversary. When recalling his time as manager at St Ives, David Leach thought that he had 'never considered myself as a potter in the individualistic sense one thinks of today, but as a member of a team at a village pottery where perhaps I could be constructive in a practical way'.[2] 'I thought little about my personal work, feeling that my first attention should be given to the building of the team and the practical establishment of the Pottery, which must combine economic stability with good craftsmanship. I thought of my father as the creative force. I had a deep urge to make my own pots but no great impatience about it.'[3]

However, in 1949, David held a substantial exhibition, his first one-person show, at Downing's Bookshop Gallery in St Ives. Here he showed some hundred pieces that included 'an elliptical vase with rust and blue decoration, a coffee set in temmoku glaze and a mottled rust and blue grey vase'.[4] Reviewing the exhibition the sculptor Barbara Hepworth was drawn to the 'alchemy ' of art, and impressed by the desire 'to bring into daily life the vital beauty of objects which are a joy to hold in the hand'.[5] After analysing various pieces on show, such

The team at the Leach Pottery, 1947. Clockwise from left, Bernard Leach, Kenneth Quick, David Leach, Joe Benny, Horatio Nelson Dunn, Mary Gibson Horrocks, in centre Aileen Newton.

David Leach, mead set, bottle and four cups, thrown and turned, stoneware, 1950. The F. F. Mead stamp indicates they were produced for Francis Fawcett, The Bedloe Winery, Buckinghamshire.

David Leach fitting a wooden tap to a cider bottle, Horatio Dunn carrying a board of pots in the background, Leach Pottery, St Ives, 1950.

as a bowl 'a perfect example of the outer and inner curve', a beer-set and a 'graceful celadon mead set', which revealed 'David Leach's fine sensibility for stance and proportion', she concluded that he was 'one of our foremost potters'. The mead set, designed and made by David, had initially been prompted by an order from Francis Fawcett, a mead-maker in High Wycombe, who wanted presentation sets for special customers. Although the exhibition was an important step in recognising David as an individual potter, it was not to be repeated for many years. 'I was not concerned at that stage with my own development as an individual potter but with the building up of a well-trained and organized team primarily concerned with the production of my father's inspirational ideas; this involved close cooperation with him over the interpretation to our team of students and apprentices of the many creative, technical and productive problems.'[6]

## In Partnership

With the partnership established, David settled down as manager, made the day-to-day decisions, but always discussed any major issues with his father. He also assisted Bernard Leach with his individual pots, ensuring that he had the help he required and that the pots were well fired. In 1950 Bernard Leach went on a four-month tour of the United States, leaving David in sole charge. Unlike an earlier visit to Scandinavia, when Laurie accompanied him, he travelled alone, an indication of the growing problems in the relationship. With the realisation that his marriage had all but ended, Bernard Leach undertook a far-reaching review of his life. Part of his long-term strategy was to make extended visits to Japan and in a complex combination of altruism and practicality he took the dramatic step of distributing his property amongst his children on the understanding that each would pay him £50 a year to provide him with an income. It was an arrangement that meant that his family could benefit from his property while he was alive rather than wait until he was dead and at the same time free him from the responsibility of ownership and death duties. David got the Pottery premises lock, stock and barrel, though his father retained Pottery Cottage, and a half share of the business itself.

In keeping with Bernard Leach's international ambitions he, together with Muriel Rose who was then working at The British Council, made a bold and radical proposal to hold a twelve-day

St Ives Pottery tableware catalogue with prices, 1954.

Cover of Leach Pottery, St Ives, catalogue featuring a mead bottle made by Bernard Leach, 1952.

31

**The Throwing Process,
Leach Pottery, St Ives, 1946**

Top left: David Leach wedging a lump of clay; above,
opening up a lump of clay on the kick wheel; left,
throwing a pot on the kick wheel.

David Leach turning a foot on a leather-hard plate on the kick wheel, Leach Pottery, St Ives, 1946.

David's eldest son, John Leach the Muchelney Potter, Somerset, 1981.

conference on pottery and textiles at Dartington Hall, reinforcing his notion of a 'world-wide outlook'.[7] Before the conference David had been in touch with Edward Burke, the chief chemist at the Portland Cement Company and himself an amateur potter, to research the possibility of a porcelain body that would fire to a delicate translucence at around 1260°-1280°C. a temperature considerably more attainable than the more usual 1400°C., which was typical of continental ware. Perhaps unsurprisingly, experiments with adding such materials as shampoo powders, proved unsuccessful, but the use of a white firing, highly plastic material called bentonite proved more promising. Ten times more plastic than ordinary ball clay, small additions of bentonite to the porcelain mixture meant that less clay needed to be used but resulted in an equally plastic and throwable body, and one that matured at a lower temperature. An unidentified Belgian potter used this modified clay to throw a fifteen-inch (380mm) bowl and a tall bottle. David continued to develop the body, which unfortunately had a tendency to slump if over fired.

With his son firmly in charge at the Pottery, his properties sorted out and encouraged by Yanagi, Bernard Leach planned a long tour of Japan. In the 1952 Pottery catalogue he indicated his confidence in his son, saying that in his absence David would assume charge with 'the opportunity to develop it in his own way now rather than later'.[8] Paradoxically this both liberated David from, and bound him to, the Leach mould, and though at first reluctant to accept the role of leader rather than manager – of the potter being an artist as well as a craftsman – he was well aware that he had 'not done very much about myself in this respect'.[9] He was equally sensitive to the fact that his respect for his father both shaped his understanding of the craft but could also be overpowering. It would, he thought, have been easier if he had reacted against it but as he found himself so often in agreement, establishing his own clear identity proved elusive. 'If a pot came out of the kiln that he thought was a beauty, well I generally thought it was a beauty too. We were in tune on values in pots and this made the establishment of my independence the more difficult.'[10]

Although all the potters at the Pottery were encouraged to make their own work, David had been reasonably content to throw some of his father's exhibition pots, and there was little motivation for him to explore his own ideas at this time; he was

David Leach teaching students at Loughborough College of Art, discussing jugs made as part of a project, 1954.

an able organiser, had considerable marketing skills, had successfully rebuilt the kiln and had a well-trained crew of experienced potters, some of whom had left to teach in the rapidly expanding pottery departments being set up in art schools. His aesthetic understanding centred around the value of functional form, the qualities of a reduction-fired clay body, and the deep beauty of classical Oriental glazes such as celadons and temmokus, while his father seemed to know instinctively what made a satisfying pot.

There was a slight breaking away when, in the autumn of 1951, he was invited to advise a recently established Pottery in the village of Kjerringvik, near Sandefjord, Norway. A German potter, Hans-Peter Pfeifer, had set up a stoneware pottery but had met with technical difficulties in the running of it. After Pfeifer had visited the Leach Pottery seeking advice, David went to Norway for six weeks to help resolve the problems.

## Teaching and Education

With such a sound understanding of all aspects of running a pottery, it was perhaps not surprising that David was approached to become involved in art school education. The first of such involvements was at Loughborough College of Art, a school with strong links with the arts and crafts tradition. This followed a poor report of the pottery teaching at the college in 1953 by Mildred Lockyer, the HMI responsible, who after studying at the Royal

College of Art, had worked at the Leach Pottery. In her view it did not meet the required standards and she recommended that a potter be appointed to run the course. The Principal, Jack Divine, who had studied ceramics with William Staite Murray at the Royal College of Art, duly spent the Easter vacation at the Leach Pottery watching the potters at work and, impressed by their skills, invited David, with his practical training, to take over the department. Although David was aware of his limited educational experience he saw this as both a challenge and a welcome opportunity to broaden his approach. A great attraction was that, much to his astonishment, the pay was three or four times more than he was earning as a potter and he agreed to take the position for an academic year from September 1953.

David's experience of education was limited to teaching children and adults at Dartington and students at Penzance Art School, but none of this was at the level expected at Loughborough. It was a position for which, while he was aware of having little academic experience, he did have a great deal of practical understanding. Nevertheless, he was obliged to learn the intricacies of Intermediate and NDD (National Diploma of Design) art examinations, barely keeping a lap ahead of the students. Although aware that art schools were more concerned with nurturing the innate creative abilities of the students rather than imposing particular concepts, he approached the teaching on the basis that they needed to learn techniques before they could evolve a style, though he was ever willing to respond to the individual needs and interests of the students in a generous and open way.[11]

After demonstrating various processes, the students were encouraged to practice basic pottery skills and under David's expert tuition achieved remarkable results. He was, remembered Bob Rogers, 'an excellent and generous teacher on the purely practical level, where his skill and meticulous craftsmanship was valued by staff and students alike. More importantly he was good at getting the students to think about what they were doing in general philosophical terms'.[12] During later visits David Leach was seen as an inspiration to many students on the studio pottery course.

The year culminated with an exhibition of David's pots shown alongside Loughborough student work at Heal and Son, in London, which was thought a great success.[13] A favourable review in Pottery Quarterly, focused on David's pots, declaring that they had 'flowered and grown in stature'[14], a response that affirmed his decision to take the teaching opportunity. Although he declined to accept a full-time commitment for a further year, he did continue to visit regularly for blocks of teaching. The trail that David had blazed so successfully was confirmed when Arthur Griffiths was appointed head of the department. After studying at Wolverhampton Art School Griffiths had also worked at the Leach Pottery and was thought a sound choice.

During David's teaching in Loughborough the day-to-day running of the Pottery was left in the collective hands of his brother Michael, Bill Marshall and Frank Vibert, the secretary and general organiser, when, in David's words, it was allowed to 'find its own feet'. It was a situation that he realised was far from satisfactory and he felt that Michael still lacked sufficient management experience and tact to be left in sole charge, but as a member of the family Michael should be involved in its management. As David was only to be absent during term time, he was able to reassume control in the long holidays. While his father saw the advantages for David in being involved in art school education, he thought David should have a full-time presence at the Pottery, and that 'remote control' would prove difficult.

At this time David's wife Elizabeth converted to Catholicism under the guidance of her brother Guy, who for a time had become a Benedictine monk at Buckfast Abbey, and a local priest Father Delaney. Following her lead David, nominally a member of the Church of England, also converted, mostly out of respect for his wife and convenience for his family, although he remained an active and committed Buchmanite. Simon, their youngest son, was brought up a Catholic, but David never felt any deep conviction, and tended to let his commitment slide, feeling that the church had been set up after Christ's death, and the competition between different sects failed to recognise the centrality of Christ himself.

Indirectly, through his Catholic faith, David accepted an invitation to establish a pottery workshop producing tableware for the Carmelite Friars at Aylesford in Kent. George and Carol Downing, who ran their bookshop in St Ives, were keen amateurs potters, and Carol, who had become a Catholic and attended a course at Aylesford, heard from the Prior, Father Malachy Lynch, that he wanted to set up a pottery, and she proposed David as someone more than able to set up such a venture. Father Malachy Lynch, who was a keen supporter of Arts and Crafts ideas, was an imposing prophet-like figure with a beaked nose and white shoulder-length hair. In addition to establishing a pottery he instigated a printing press, which was also intended to be a creative activity for the Brothers.

It was another challenge David relished, albeit one that again took him away from the Pottery. For the first six months at Aylesford he made and fired slipware, thrown and moulded, in an electric kiln. Aware that he had agreed only to set up, rather than manage, the Pottery, he invited the young potter Colin Pearson to take over as resident potter.[15] At this point David designed a scaled down version of the stoneware kiln at St Ives, with only two chambers half the size of the original and with Pearson's help built the oil-fired kiln. Initially this proved temperamental with uneven temperature front to back, which took time to sort out. In addition to tableware, David was also asked to produce a selection of 'Catholic pottery', such as Holy water stoops, candlesticks and items required for use within the community. Much of the pottery's output was used in the Friary but it was also sold to the many visiting pilgrims to raise funds. The scheme again meant long periods when David was away from St Ives, which, together with his father's absence in Japan, led the crew to feel that the Pottery was suffering from a lack of clear direction. With the Aylesford Pottery up and running in the capable hands of Colin Pearson, David returned every six months to check on production and see the young potter, his visits welcomed for his enthusiasm and generosity.

Late in 1954 Bernard Leach came back from Japan with plans to return within a year leaving the Pottery in David's hands. In Japan Bernard Leach had formed a relationship with a young American potter named Janet Darnell and, after divorcing Laurie, intended to go back, marry Janet and set up a pottery. But friends in Japan advised him that moving permanently to the country would be difficult, and Leach felt that he had to radically revise his plans. Accepting that he could not now settle with Janet in Japan, Bernard told David that he intended to remain at St Ives and that Janet Darnell would join him as his wife and partner. This was the last thing that David expected, for he was now looking forward to being in sole charge and he felt both 'a big disappointment' and 'an instinctive negative reaction'.[16] Practically he was doubtful if such an arrangement would work and emotionally he was reluctant to share the Pottery with another unknown potter who was so closely involved with his father. In the end he felt he had no option but to leave and establish his own pottery. 'It was', he recalled 'a big, awkward, embarrassing decision but one which I felt I must make.'[17]

The decision crystallised many of David's thoughts about establishing a career that was independent of his father. 'I was becoming increasingly aware of my own limited development, of an uncomfortable frustrating realisation of something my father had reiterated down these formative years: – "That in the world of today a craftsman must needs be artist too."'[18] Although initially apprehensive about taking over at St Ives, he had now warmed to the challenge, and this was about to be taken away. Leaving the Pottery would not only be an opportunity to set up his own workshop, but also to establish his own home, which with two children and a third expected, (Simon Andrew, was born in 1956) both he and Elizabeth felt it was timely. Using his inheritance from his mother, who had died in 1955, he acquired a large Edwardian house with a pottery studio at Lowerdown Cross, Bovey Tracey in south Devon, although in view of Elizabeth's pregnancy it was decided to delay their departure until after the birth. For David it was the start of an independent career and the opportunity to establish his own voice as a potter.[19]

**FOOTNOTES**

1. For a full account of the Leach Pottery in the early 1950s see Murray Fieldhouse 'Workshop visit to Leach Pottery', *Pottery Quarterly: A Review of Ceramic Art*, vol. 1, no. 1, Spring 1954.

2. David Leach in Robert Fournier, *David Leach: A Potter's Life: with Workshop Notes*, Lacock, second edition, 1979, page 10.

3. Murray Fieldhouse, 'Workshop Visit – the Leach Pottery', *Pottery Quarterly: A Review of Ceramic Art*, vol. 1, no. 1, Spring 1954.

4. 'The Potter's Craft', *The Cornishman*, August 18, 1949.

5. 'David Leach: The Importance of Form and Colour', *The St Ives Times*, August 19, 1949.

6. David Leach, 'Lowerdown Pottery', *Ceramic Review*, May/June, number 21, 1973. pp'. 4-7.

7. Its broad scope also fitted in with Bernard Leach's plans to spend time in Japan. The international conference and exhibition had the broad aim of considering the role of the craftsman and woman in the post-war world, and to offer a global perspective that would consider practical, aesthetic and educational issues. The conference also looked to alert a new generation of the hard-won inter-war achievements. Unlike contemporary painters and sculptors, who tended to look to America for modern developments, makers of woven textiles turned to Scandinavia while potters, at least those of concern to Leach, looked east, and this was how the programme was drawn up. The international twelve-day conference, and accompanying exhibition that subsequently toured round Britain, was ambitious and wide-ranging. Over a hundred delegates came from the USA, Europe, Asia and Africa as well as Yanagi and Hamada from Japan, the event blending entertainment, stimulation and information, when potters and weavers discussed shared objectives, considered new developments and the uneasy relationship between craft and industry.

8. Bernard Leach, *Leach Pottery 1920-1952*, Pamphlet, St Ives, 1952. Family archives.

9. Fournier, page 13.

10. *ibid.*

11. I am indebted to Bob and Mary Rogers for an account of David Leach's time at Loughborough.

12. Letter to Emmanuel Cooper from Bob and Mary Rogers, 29 August 2002.

13. David Leach did well at Loughborough, the students holding a much-acclaimed end of year show at Heals in Tottenham Court Road, London, which was opened by Lady Isabel Barnett.

14. 'Pottery from Loughborough College', Heal's, October. *Pottery Quarterly: A Review of Ceramic Art*, Winter, 1955, no. 4.

15. Colin Pearson had worked with Ray Finch at Winchcombe Pottery and was highly recommended by him.

16. Interview with author, 31 October 1996.

17. David Leach, 'Lowerdown Pottery', *Ceramic Review*, May/June, number 21, 1973. pp. 4-7.

18. *ibid.*

19. Michael also left at this time, setting up his pottery in north Devon.

# Chapter Four
# 'The Craftsman's Way of Life', South Devon, 1955-

The home David Leach had built in 1969 at Lowerdown, 2002.

## Lowerdown

Set within striking distance of Dartmoor and well away from the main highways leading to the west, Lowerdown Cross, half a mile from the town of Bovey Tracey in south Devon was, and still is, delightfully unspoilt; the narrow roads and tall hedges have a timeless, ancient feel, well suited to the quiet production of a small studio workshop. Unlike the austerity of the wind-blown hills of Cornwall, this part of the West Country is lush and verdant, with houses nestling comfortably in the welcoming, rolling landscape. In spring 1956, shortly after the birth of David and Elizabeth's third child, Simon, the family moved to Devon and quickly settled into the large and comfortable house with its extensive garden.

The Ehlers, from whom the house was purchased, were friends of the potter Lucie Rie, and like her were Jewish refugees. Lily was a potter and for a period after the war she had helped Lucie Rie to make ceramic buttons for the fashion industry. Alfred Ehlers was a scientist, who had worked in the aircraft industry devising special paints, but in the early fifties he developed a serious illness from the fumes and it was decided to put the house on the market. David Leach acquired the extensive property, which included a pottery studio complete with electric kiln (24x30x30ins [61x76x76cms] deep), for £5000.[1] David had met the Ehlers's daughter, Marion, at the 1952 Dartington Conference and visited her parents and in consequence was familiar with their house.

While the children were growing up the large house was eminently suitable, but as the boys left home David and Elizabeth began to make plans to move into a smaller and easier to maintain property. At the end of the sixties they commissioned a young architect, Ann Horlock Stringer, who was married to the potter Harry Horlock Stringer, to design a spacious modern house that was to be built in the grounds, and on completion the old house was to be sold. The new, modern-style house was a great contrast to the rambling Edwardian property; it was open plan, airy and spacious with large, full-length windows; in many ways it reflected the new identity David was creating for himself.

## The Pottery

For David Leach, setting up his own pottery and virtually restarting his career as an independent potter in his mid-forties represented both a challenge – in devising a range of work that was to be identifiably his – and an opportunity to establish himself as a potter in his own right. While feeling more than competent as a practical potter, he was aware that, having worked with his father, he had absorbed his aesthetic and artistic judgements, but was without the general art training that was, for most potters, the starting point in developing their own ideas. However, with experience of teaching at Loughborough and setting up the pottery studio at Aylesford, David Leach was undaunted and, needing an income, started production as soon as possible. The fact that the property was already equipped with a pottery studio – set up in a spacious corrugated shed – meant that he could begin making within the existing premises and with minimal changes. Knowing that direct selling was by far the most effective and remunerative, in 1967 he built a showroom at the front of the workshop, which allowed the public to see and to purchase a good selection of pots.

Like other studio potters working at the time such as Harry Davis at Crowan Pottery in Cornwall, Ray Finch at Winchcombe, Gloucestershire, and Geoffrey Whiting at Avoncroft Pottery in Worcestershire, David aimed to supply domestic ware that was a real alternative to industrially produced pots. They had to be well made and designed with a real sense of the personality of the potter providing individual style. Perhaps significantly, Davis, Finch and Whiting had either trained at the Leach Pottery or had been greatly influenced by Bernard Leach's ideas, each interpreting them in their own way. All shared an interest in focusing production on high-quality functional

David Leach, two earthenware bottles with sgraffito decoration, Lowerdown Pottery, 1958.

tableware sold at a relatively modest price while making more expensive individual pots alongside. These pots were seen as a natural extension of the tableware into more decorative pieces in which function was less of a consideration than the harmonious use of form, decoration and material.

## Apprentices, assistants and production

Preferring to work in a small team, David Leach continued the concept he had started at St Ives of working with and training young potters, taking on a variety of assistants that ranged from apprentices who stayed two or three years to acquire a full craft training alongside short- and long-term assistants, and students who wanted experience of working in a highly successful production pottery. These included students from Britain and overseas, keen to get practical experience, some of whom worked during college vacations. Despite the relatively short time they were at the Pottery, the first-hand involvement of the day-to-day life of an industrious workshop was invaluable.

As a result, the pots produced fell into three types; those made entirely by a student or assistant, those made by David Leach alone, and some that were a combined effort, maybe thrown by a student and decorated or fluted by David. There were different seals for each type to distinguish them. David Leach's individual seal is a small D inside a large L, set within either a square or a circle. The pottery stamp is a large L with a small + in a circle, denoting Lowerdown Cross.

The assistants and apprentices who stayed for two or even three years became an essential part of the production team. They received not only a thorough practical training in mixing bodies, making, glazing and firing pots but also took part in wider discussions about the life of the potter and the sort of qualities to look for in successful pots, debate that for many of them was just as valuable as the practical training. It is a mark of David Leach's skill, enthusiasm and openness that of all the assistants and apprentices who worked with him none simply went on to emulate his style, but later developed their own highly individual work, some focusing on one-off pieces, others on producing domestic tableware as well as individual pots.

The well-structured working day was similar to that which David established at St Ives. It began at 8.30am and in the winter

Tim Andrews while a student-apprentice at Lowerdown Pottery beside the oil-fired kiln starting to unpack it, 1978.

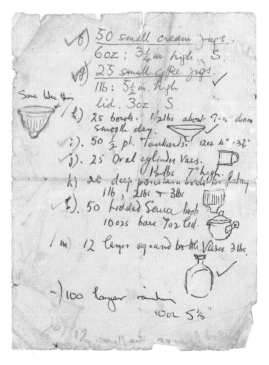

Tim Andrews' work sheet, Lowerdown Pottery, c.1978.

the first task was to light the small wood-burning stove; this not only heated the workshop but was also used to boil kettles and dry off pots. Logs would be split for kindling and a fire laid and set. In winter the timber and corrugated iron building, with large garage doors, was difficult to keep warm, but ideal when the warmer weather came. The workshop rhythm revolved around the regular firings of the large kiln, with three or four weeks of making followed by a week or so of decorating and glazing, kiln packing and firing. Each week David Leach wrote out the making list to suit orders and shapes needed for the kiln. Apprentices were given a clear idea of what was expected, or at least what to aim for.

Well-aged clay was wedged, carefully weighed and balled up, with quantities varying from fifty to a hundred depending on the item being made. Pots were usually made on a Leach kick wheel, with David Leach first throwing a sample, pointing out the most efficient making sequence and warning of some of the pitfalls. After a while he would return with a jovial 'are you any good today?'[2] Tim Andrews found David Leach an accomplished and sensitive teacher, knowing when to intervene and when to hold back, a skill that looked deceptively easy but one that called on a wealth of experience and a shrewd awareness of the student's strengths and weaknesses. David Leach's comments on pots might involve observations such as 'that one looks a little down on its heels', or

David Leach throwing a bottle, with John Maltby to his right. Note the row of fired teapots and the unfired coffee pots, Lowerdown Pottery, 1963.

'straighten that line a little to get some life' – all important ways of 'reading' and understanding form. There was no radio in the workshop, but occasionally an old gramophone would appear and David Leach would play recordings of Paul Robeson spirituals.

At eleven there was a fifteen-minute break for coffee and two plain biscuits, and in winter a chat round the stove. Lunch was from one to two; there was tea in the afternoon and the day finished at six. Break-time conversations were an opportunity for discussion, whether on purely practical matters or considerations of more philosophical issues.

The first assistant was Freda Sage, who arrived in 1957, having had useful potting experience with Marianne de Trey who had a pottery in nearby Dartington. At Lowerdown, Sage was involved in establishing the new range of earthenware at which she excelled and soon became the mainstay in the production of domestic work. She was especially adept at making a variety of moulded dishes for which she devised a range of decorative motifs based on flowers and plants. Sage stayed for three years, living as a member of the family.[3]

Shortly after setting up, the team at Lowerdown was joined by David Leach's eldest son, John, who wanted to learn the craft. He remained for a full three-year apprenticeship before going to work for his grandfather, Bernard, at the Leach Pottery. In 1964 he set up his own workshop, Muchelney Pottery in Somerset, where he quickly gained a reputation for his generously rounded hand-thrown kitchen stoneware characterised by its unglazed 'toasted' wood-fired finish. John Maltby, who had studied sculpture at Leicester School of Art, also came to Lowerdown to become a potter. In time Maltby became a skilled thrower and a valued member of the team, leaving to set up his own pottery at Stoneshill, Devon, in 1965, where he produced oxidised and reduction fired stoneware. Other long-term assistants followed, including Warwick Parker, Jeremy Leach, David Leach's second son and Simon Leach, his youngest son. In the summer months students were taken for short periods to gain direct experience of a production workshop. A stream of assistants and helpers were a regular part of the team until the late 1980s, when the production of tableware was giving way to more individual pieces.

David Leach (centre) watching his son Jeremy throw on the kick wheel, Richard Brooks, Australian student, on right, Lowerdown Pottery, 1973.

David Leach, four dishes, earthenware with slip trailed decoration under clear and green glazes, length about 200mm, Lowerdown Pottery, 1958.

## Production

Without a wood- or oil-fired reduction kiln, David started by producing a range of earthenware pots, firing them in the seven cubic foot electric kiln left behind by the Ehlers. This kiln was subsequently augmented with a top-loading Briscesco kiln. While intended only as a short-term measure to ensure a source of income, the earthenware was also a useful way of distancing himself from the range of high-fired wares so closely associated with the output at St Ives. However, while continuing to produce pots that in some ways were a continuation of those made at St Ives, he gradually evolved his own style. 'The change in my work', he recalls, 'was not the big reaction it might have been but was an evolving variation which has resulted in a quite different product from that now made at St Ives.'

The pots were mostly intended for use in the home and were either thrown on the wheel or made by pressing decorated slabs of clay over biscuit-fired moulds. Two distinct types were produced – slip-decorated terracotta and tin-glazed pots. The slipware mostly consisted of pressed dishes decorated with different earth-coloured slips including white, cream, tan and black poured or trailed under a clear lead glaze, which in one sense harked back to the slipware made at St Ives before 1937. The oblong dishes with rounded corners were given a neat, piecrust decoration round the edge, which was left unglazed. This contrasted with the quiet repeating patterns of the slip decoration and the shiny clear glaze. Crisply made, the dishes combined an awareness of tradition but set within a modern aesthetic.

David Leach, pot, earthenware, thrown with painted black glaze unglazed red clay surface, h.380mm, d.460mm, c.1960.

In contrast to the rural look of the slip-decorated ware, the tin-glazed ware was more sophisticated and modern in feel. The sparkling quality of the white glaze gave the pots a look that was clear and fresh. The glaze contained 10% of tin oxide, which when applied over a black manganese slip producing a soft grey colour with a subtle speckle. Decoration with sgraffito patterns and linear engraving was minimal and low-key, perfectly matching the strong forms. The result was an attractive, quietly textured surface, which, while making no attempt to emulate the look of stoneware, had a similar depth and subtlety.

Like much of David Leach's work it was characterised by its skilful finish and well-placed and efficient handles. The consistent and coherent range included casseroles, plates, bowls, coffee pots, jugs and jam pots. While echoing some of the shapes made at St Ives, the distinctive glaze and minimal decoration gave it a highly unusual appearance. When planning the shapes David Leach drew on long discussions with his father about what made a 'good pot', interpreting this in anthropomorphic terms, attributing it with a neck, shoulder, belly and foot, all of which should form a coherent whole.

Familiar with the outlets around the country that sold Leach Pottery standard ware, David approached them with a view to them taking his new earthenware. He received a positive response; they liked the new work and placed orders. As much of it as possible, however, was sold directly to the public. Despite David's initial doubts, the earthenware proved popular; the pots with the speckled tin glaze had a resonance with the simplicity of Scandinavian ceramics, were reasonably priced and marked a change from the pots he made at St Ives. Production of earthenware continued until 1961.

David Leach standing in front of the oil-fired kiln, Lowerdown Pottery, c.1963.

David Leach, coffee set, stoneware with matt speckled glaze and painted iron decoration, 1983.

## Stoneware

In 1960, feeling sufficiently well established and following the success of the earthenware, David Leach carried out his original intention of moving to high-temperature firing and, over a twelve-month period, he planned and built a stoneware kiln. The semi-continuous down draught, two-chamber kiln had a packing chamber of seventy cubic feet, and was fired with a single oil burner. The size was geared to regular production with a small team of potters, and when the Pottery was in full spate it was fired roughly once a month.

With the completion of the kiln in 1961 earthenware was abandoned in favour of stoneware. As far as the shapes were concerned, moving to high-temperature ware involved only a small amount of redesigning as the sound, functional forms lent themselves to the different type of firing that stoneware required, but with different glazes the pots took on other qualities. In many ways the range was typical of domestic tableware made in the 1960s; it was carefully potted and thoughtfully designed, and informed by an ethos that was about producing a viable, well-priced, attractive and functional ware. While similar to the earthenware shapes, the stoneware pots conveyed wholeness and robust health; it was solid without being heavy, and crisp without looking slick. As far as design was concerned, emphasis was on simplicity with the natural characteristics of the clay being allowed to give the pieces a warm, friendly quality.

David Leach, lidded coffee pot with dark celadon glaze, stoneware, thrown and turned, Lowerdown Pottery, h.178mm, c.1970.

David Leach, lidded storage pot, temmoku glaze, stoneware, thrown and turned, Lowerdown Pottery, c.1970.

The majority of the tableware was thrown using a tough, medium-coloured brown body made up of ball clays with 15% sand, which flashed an attractive toasted colour on unglazed areas. Full use was made of the contrast between glaze, body and decoration. The range of shapes included coffee and tea sets, a selection of casseroles, plates, mugs, jugs, bowls, basins and ramekins. Typical of the pieces made were coffee pots with matching milk jug and sugar basin. With a perky thrown handle attached on the side, the jugs took on an almost continental feeling, though the muted glazes were part of what had become an English tradition. A favourite glaze had a matt oatmeal finish, with soft iron speckles breaking through the surface. Other favourite glazes included a pale green celadon and a rich black-brown temmoku.

One of the characteristics of the ware was the use of decoration, which set it apart from the more austere forms made at St Ives. While the range of motifs was, as David Leach says 'not very exploratory', it was vigorous and related well to the form. One of the most popular designs, and one which David continues to use, consists of a brushed plant-like motif derived from foxgloves that embodies an alive, growing quality. The broad leaf-like forms that make up the base contrast pleasantly with the more delicate elongated flower-like shapes. It is a motif that David returns to in many variations; it can readily be fitted on to shapes as diverse as bowls, flat plates and bottles.

Although it was inevitable that the design of the tableware owed some allegiance to that produced at St Ives, it was and is, nevertheless, very distinctively Lowerdown. Overall the shapes are softer, slightly more relaxed, and the decoration – a skill that David discovered came almost naturally to him – is easier, more fulsome and flamboyant. In addition to painted or trailed decoration, he also developed a facility for fluting the sides of pots, a process that calls for a steady hand and a calm inner spirit, particularly when a large bowl may involve about one hundred flutes and all must form part of a rhythm that echoes and flows into a whole. David Leach became highly skilled in the technique. 'What I aim for is integration between the deeply cut, sharp-edged foot and the flutes', he says, 'which I vary in sharpness and width and complement with different glazes, some shiny, some gently breaking the surface, some muted, as in recent experiments with gun-metal glaze.'[4]

David Leach in the showroom at Lowerdown Pottery, illustrating the wide range of pots produced, c.1970.

The technique involves using various homemade tools, some made out of steel, others out of a sharpened bamboo tool to shave off narrow bands of clay down the side to leave slight ridges, which are picked up by the glaze. The various tools give different results; broader ones give cuts that are more and more pronounced, narrower ones producing quieter and more understated marks. Fluting is often carried out while the pot is being 'nursed' on his lap, a delicate activity in which precision and assurance must be combined with freedom. The cuts are especially effective under a temmoku glaze that flows slightly during the firing leaving the lines a bright orange where the glaze runs thinner. These contrast with the deep mirror-black where the glaze is thicker. On more recent pieces David has developed a darker, slightly matt dark glaze that also breaks well over the fluting.

Some of David Leach's strongest and most admired pieces are his teapots, forms that are recognisably his. Most, though not all, are rounded and full-bodied, with a thrown, narrow, tapering spout that pours well and seems to grow from the centre of the pot. The well-fitting lid, whether in the form of a cap or in a neat gallery, is held firmly in place when the pot is in use. Many of his teapots are topped off with a cane handle. With four different components – body, spout, handle and lid – the teapot calls for a unity between all the parts, a coming together in one well-balanced whole. With an acute sense of what is appropriate, a David Leach teapot – an object that he sees as 'hedged about with functional aspects' – is a pleasing balance between style, decoration and use. Despite making many teapots over the years, he says that he is 'still left with a vast opportunity to experiment with form and relationship, which can serve function without being a part of it'.

Such creative interpretation is very evident if teapots made by David Leach are placed side by side, for although they all share a common language, each one has its own subtly different character. A photograph taken in the early 1960s shows John Maltby, then an apprentice, working alongside David with a row of teapots in the background, and though all were thrown at the same time, each has its own qualities (page 41).

## Firing

With a full team the Pottery worked in approximately three- or four-weekly cycles for firing the large kiln, while biscuit firings, to

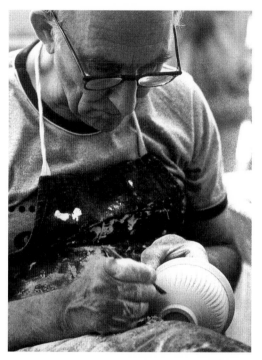

David Leach fluting a porcelain bowl, resting the pot on his knee, 1991.

960°C, were done regularly in three electric kilns all different in size and firing cycle. After a few weeks of making, the biscuit-fired pots were glazed, mostly by dipping or pouring and after being decorated were prepared for firing. Packing required knowledge of the kiln and the different glazes, some of which matured at slightly higher or lower temperatures and so could be suited to the unevenness of the kiln temperature from top to bottom. After boards of pots were identified and labelled with their glaze, the kiln pack was planned. As far as possible all the available space would be used, with an eggcup or an extra bottle vase being squeezed in whenever possible. When packed the kiln door was built up of a jigsaw of bricks, which were clammed up using old clay and floor sweepings.

Often only one of the two chambers of the kiln was used. At other times, dependent on the type of work and the productive capacity of the team, both chambers were packed. The firing temperature was about 1300°C. On average around 800 pots were produced from each firing. The kiln has what David described as 'an incorrigible temperature difference of about 40°C., part of the devil I had to get used to, and so different glazes were used to accommodate this variation'. The temmoku and ash glazes fired in the region of 1300°C., while the celadons, dolomites and titania glazes together with the porcelain at the lower range between 1270°C. and 1280°C. This was turned into a positive advantage in that it afforded more variety, but a 40°C difference meant that at 1310°C., the body was all but over-fired while at 1260°C it was nearing a slight porosity.

The kiln was gently warmed up over night and the firing proper started the next morning. The first chamber reached temperature in about thirteen and a half hours, the second – partially with the use of wood – in a further six, making a total of nearly twenty hours. The slow heat was followed with a faster oxidising atmosphere until 900°C. plus, when a period of soak ensured that carbonaceous matter would burn out and so prevent bloating later. Reduction and a slow climb to 1300°C. followed. At top temperature the kiln was soaked to even out the temperature and a final period of oxidation finished the firing. When the first chamber had reached temperature, the second chamber was around 800°C. and was taken up by side-stoking with wood.

David Leach decorating standard ware with iron brush decoration, Lowerdown Pottery, c.1970.

David Leach, tea set with foxglove decoration, c.1985.

David Leach painting a porcelain bowl, 1989.

Immediately the kiln had reached temperature it was fast-cooled with cold air running from the open fire-mouth through chamber one until the pyrometer had dropped to 700°C. in about four hours. The chimney dampers were then closed to impede the flow of cold air. A blissful silence followed when the air blower was turned off.

A firing consumed approximately thirty to thirty-five gallons of gas oil and three barrow loads of preferably resinous pinewood. For decades at St Ives and at Lowerdown, David preferred to be in charge of the firing, and was always distrustful to 'delegate this midwife's duty to another'. Difficult kilns are notoriously long to learn, and he felt an intimacy that grew over the years between a fireman and his kiln that 'required a tuned ear to its merest whimper or cry in the lonely dark of the night'. When Simon Leach worked for his father, he was particularly gratified when, during one of his father's workshop visits abroad he was left with responsibility to pack and fire the kiln, a firing which proved highly successful, despite the complicated packing and nursing process.

Like most potters, David Leach was, and still is, keen to unpack the kiln and examine the results. Ever impatient to see how the firing had gone, he approached the large kiln gingerly the following day and, despite the great heat, would prise out the top brick on the door to take a peep. Gradually pieces were removed, often by using a pocket handkerchief, and on more than one occasion there was a crash followed by shouting as a particularly hot pot slipped and landed on a pile of other pots.

**FOOTNOTES**

1. Alfred Ehlers died in March 1956. Lily Ehlers and her daughter moved to Lyme Regis.
2. Many thanks to Tim Andrews for providing a full account of his apprenticeship with David Leach, which started in 1976.
3. After leaving Lowerdown Freda Sage taught at Ipswich School of Art where she met Beryl Debeny, who had studied under Dick Kendall at Camberwell School of Art.
4. David Leach, *Crafts* Magazine, May/June 1979, page 35.

## Chapter Five
# Elegance and Strength – The Individual Pots

'As a potter rather than a technologist I am always looking for the whole integrated pot. Good design, simple, direct, but skilled making, complimentary glaze and decoration. No virtuosity, or integrated eye-catching deviations',[1] is typical of David Leach's philosophy, whether referring to domestic tableware but more especially with regard to his individual or one-off pieces. At Lowerdown, David had welcomed the opportunity to be a potter in 'his own right' and on his own terms. Over the years he has become more and more involved with making one-off pieces, leaving his assistants to produce much of the standard ware, though he also continued to make it when necessary and is always on hand to check its quality.

Wary of describing his one-off pots as 'individual', he prefers to see them as part of a family of forms that are continually reinterpreted. 'As far as the shapes are concerned', he says, 'they are tentatively made and are put into the kiln to see what happens. I make similar shapes over and over again, so that while each one is individual they are in a style and convention that involves variations on a theme.'

At the heart of his work lies a deep understanding of the materials and how they behave in the kiln. 'I learnt', he says, 'never to be put off when making anything, but to respond to the behaviour of the materials and to recognise that constant reassessment of one's work is the essential process of growth.'[2] He is also aware that

David Leach decorating a bottle during a demonstration, c.1975.

potters are freer to experiment than many other craftsmen and women in that they can discard pots that have not come up to standard. 'The materials we use are cheap, the making process is relatively quick, and we can try out ideas, this freedom is virtually unique to the potter.'[3]

With regard to his forms, David Leach is conscious of avoiding those that might be too close to his father's pots while at the same time accepting that his interest also lies in work that owes much to classic oriental shapes and the deep, rich glazes such as celadon and temmoku. He could not nor did he particularly wish to start looking at other sources, and from the early days at Lowerdown realised that his own style would develop slowly.

## Stoneware

In his one-off pieces David concentrates on a range of forms that includes rounded bottles, jars and dishes in stoneware, lidded boxes and bowls. The smaller bottles are thrown in a single piece, the larger are often thrown in two or three parts; in some the main body is completed first and the neck thrown separately and joined later. Taller shapes are joined in the middle. Adding the neck involves assessing the shape in relation to the body, with consideration given to its size, the thickness of the rim, and whether it should be rounded or cut so that it feels and looks right.

On some bottles David applies bold, iron decoration, either painted with a brush or achieved by pulling his fingers through a layer of wet slip. Such movement often appears to flow down the pot adding a Zen-like point of definition that sets up a subtle and understated contrast with the temmoku glaze. On others he animates the surface with a brushed variation of the foxglove plant motif, carefully gearing it to the form of the pot. This is carried out in a pigment made up of fine ilmenite and china clay that fires a rich golden brown against the black glaze.[4] This decoration is particularly handsome, and caught the eye of the critic and collector W.A. Ismay who saw such pots as having 'great presence'.[5] Some pieces are enhanced by delicate cutting and engraving which, while making us aware of the surface, is well integrated into the form.

A relaxed decorator, David has developed a range of techniques that involve wax resist, a process in which the hot wax is painted over a slip or a glaze; this resists a further layer of the same or a different glaze. The technique of painting the hot wax has much in common with slip-trailing in that the patterns have to be bold and decisive as the wax dries quickly on the brush, and once applied can only be removed with great difficulty. When a wax pattern is painted over a temmoku glaze or a black slip and covered with an opaque, white, unctuous glaze the result can be dramatic as the black breaks through the upper glaze creating an almost volcanic-like surface, but one that is smoothed over and well-integrated into the form.

At their best the bottles have a self-confidence and assurance, with a sense of inner volume that sets up a tension between the expanding form and the space around it. Some of the taller forms are flattened on opposing sides, others on four sides, creating surfaces that are ideal for decoration. Such pieces are about line, volume and colour rather than function or purpose, and confirm Herbert Read's observation that pottery is the most abstract of the arts.

## Porcelain, 'a natural gift'

Just as he had been developing a translucent porcelain body at St Ives through investigating the use of bentonite, at Lowerdown David Leach continued to experiment to produce a body that became translucent without slumping. Gradually he perfected a new, workable body, which was more plastic to handle, and whilst translucent was also more reliable when fired. He published details of the body in *Ceramic Review*[6], and a version of this was prepared and commercially sold by Podmore and Co, (now Potterycrafts), a Stoke-on-Trent based company supplying craft potters as well as industrial manufacturers. David Leach also devised for Podmore a range of classic stoneware glazes such as a temmoku, celadon and oatmeal for use in reduction-fired kilns, so making them readily available to a wider range of potters.

With the new, more translucent, porcelain capable of being thrown very much thinner without distortion and which could be fired alongside the stoneware, David Leach had found his element, eventually deciding that, as 'a much more precise potter' than his father, he was 'more of a porcelain potter than a stoneware one'.[7] His father had worked initially with porcelain in the East where it tended to be more thickly rather than thinly potted, and so he regarded it more as a fine, dense white body rather than one that fired to a soft translucence. As a result, forms tended to be more robust and solid. By contrast David Leach aimed for a finer quality. In looking for lightness, his approach followed a more European ideal in being orientated to a thinner, more delicately potted material, which could exploit its translucent quality and the way in which light could affect the form. 'To me translucence has always been an essential characteristic of porcelain whether it is the limited translucence only obtained at the thinner edge of thicker walled pieces or the fuller translucence when the wall is quite thin as in the beautifully engraved Y'ing Ching porcelain of Song dynasty China.'[8]

Aware of his father's watchful eye, David Leach knew that Bernard tended to be critical of what he saw 'as my over-involvement with porcelain', and that he thought that it would make his son's work 'tight and meticulous instead of free and relaxed'. David Leach's response was to think that 'he may have been right'[9], but he also knew that he was fascinated by working with the material and discovering its qualities. Initially the proportion of porcelain produced at Lowerdown was small, amounting to only about 5% of output, but this has gradually increased as David Leach responded to its virtues, affirming his father's opinion that he looked 'for delicacy and thinness, and I think, of all these techniques, porcelain is the nearest to his natural gift'.[10]

David Leach, teacup and saucer, thrown and turned, porcelain, Lowerdown Pottery, h.64mm, demonstrating the translucency of the body, c.1975.

David Leach, porcelain 'egg', thrown and turned with crackle glaze, h. about 190mm Lowerdown Pottery, c.1980.

David Leach blowing a wet porcelain 'egg', for the final shaping of the form, c.1980.

David Leach with white lipstick resulting from blowing into the wet porcelain 'egg', c.1980.

Far from using porcelain only as a material for 'one-off' pieces, David Leach most famously produces tea sets, often finished with a pale blue Y'Ching glaze, sometimes described by him as being like 'the sky after rain'. The shapes are delicately thrown and fluted, including the teapot, the teacups, sugar basin and milk jug, beautifully marrying form and decoration. The effect is one of refinement and sophistication achieved not through the use of moulds or mechanical means, but by hand making. The slight unevenness of the fluting has a 'humanising' quality, which celebrates the qualities of the material and the process.

In her definitive book *The Crafts in Britain in the 20th Century*, Tanya Harrod wrote that it 'would be difficult to better the design of his production wares, in particular his fluted porcelain tea and coffee services'. This view was also that of Contemporary Applied Arts when, in 1987, they ran a scheme called *Art Means Business*. This was aimed mainly at corporate clients, and the publicity stressed that crafts represented a 'viable long-term investment'. This was further exemplified in the 1987 Crafts Council/Business Design Centre exhibition Top Office, consisting of a series of speculative offices created for 'Top People'. Prime Minister Margaret Thatcher's 'office', included a David Leach porcelain tea set that stood happily alongside ultra-smart designer furniture.

Of all his individual porcelain forms, one of David Leach's signature pieces is the 'egg', a rounded thrown bottle form with a narrow base and a small opening at the neck. The full, swelling form is exactly as its name suggests, an ovoid resembling an egg. The full, bursting shape has the widest part just above the waist while the narrow, almost hidden foot appears to make the piece float. 'Its form is like a Barbara Hepworth sculpture, very simple, and literally blown up on the wheel...The pot's formal tension is its essence, hence it is more successful in stoneware... than porcelain, which tends to sag, since it melts during the firing', wrote David in 1979, pointing out that of all the pots he made, this one 'bears the least relation to function'.[11]

Thrown on the wheel and all but joined up at the neck, the final tension in the piece is achieved by literally blowing into the pot while it is still on the wheel, a process that, much to David Leach's amusement, leaves a ring of white clay lipstick round his mouth. The 'eggs' are finished with a smooth matt magnesium glaze which, when the pot is removed hot from the kiln, is rubbed with fine iron oxide that enters the slight crazing on the surface giving it a fine crackle pattern. The thickness of glaze application and the firing temperature control the size of the crackle. Unique among David Leach's forms, the egg has an austerity and simplicity that relies on form rather than decoration, and though the crackle patterning locates it in an Oriental rather than a Western aesthetic, the shape has what Clive Bell might have described as 'significant form' in relating to both craft and sculpture.

David Leach's porcelain bowls are finely thrown and each has a crisply turned narrow foot, which achieve a balance between lightness, stability and strength. The outsides of some bowls are fluted, the porcelain lending itself to fine, delicate linear cuts. Unlike stoneware, the porcelain body leaves no burrs or roughened edges but cuts clean and crisp. On some bowls a soft velvety glaze is used, which enhances the form, the non-reflective surface appearing an intrinsic part of the shape and giving it a stone-like quality. On others a clear-firing pale blue glaze is used, which is particularly effective on the fluted bowls as the colour is intensified in the grooves of the fluting.

Apart from the fluting, all David Leach's decorative techniques are carried out rapidly and without hesitation, whether painting with pigment, trailing slip or cutting or scratching into the clay surface. A favourite form of decoration is a painted design recalling an abstracted landscape, a series of 'leaping' waves or in some arrangements an abstracted design of reeds and flowers, often placed at an angle running up the side of the pot. Even when carried out as brushwork it looks, says David Leach, 'as if it might have come from the nozzle of a slip trailer'. Painting may involve two pigments – a slate blue and deep iron-brown – the decoration carried out with Japanese brushes that he prefers because they give a better calligraphic quality, allow a variation in thickness whilst holding a sufficient amount of pigment but also because they have a much springier quality than European brushes other than sable. The decoration is often finished by dots of bright red or orange glaze achieved by mixing equal parts of an iron-bearing clay and nepheline syentite. The result is lively and playful, a perfect foil to the formality of the form.

Similar decoration is used on the small lidded pots, beautifully crafted objects that sensitively exploit the qualities of

David Leach, tall faceted stoneware vase, h.253mm, 1994.

David Leach, stoneware jug of medieval inspiration, variegated temmoku glaze, 1989.

David Leach, moulded slipware dishes, length 153mm, 1958.

David Leach, brown stoneware flanged bowl, engraved temmoku, 1995.

David Leach, faceted stoneware resist glaze jar, 1995.

the material. Made either in the form of a flattened egg resembling a pebble, or with straight sides and a domed lid, they vary in size from six to nine or ten centimetre in diameter. Part of the quality of these pots is the precision of their making, with a carefully turned foot and the neatly fitting lids an intrinsic part of their aesthetic appeal. Although the lid and body are thrown separately they are both carefully turned to form a snug fit and look as if they had been made as a whole, so complete do they seem. In an acute insight into his individual porcelain and stoneware in 1979 David described them as 'a balance between femininity and masculinity', saying they combine 'elegance and strength'.

David Leach and Tim Andrews at work at Lowerdown Pottery, 1990.

**FOOTNOTES**

1. David Leach, 'Lowerdown Pottery', *Ceramic Review*, May/June, number 21, 1973, pp. 4-7.

2. David Leach, *Crafts* Magazine, May/June, 1979, page 36.

3. *Ibid*.

4. The combination is one quarter china clay, the rest ilmenite. The clay helps to stop the design spreading and so retains its definition.

5. W.A. Ismay, 'David Leach: Cider Press Gallery, Dartington, 1977', *Ceramic Review*, July/August, number 46, 1977.

6. See *Ceramic Review* number 2, April 1970, pages 5-6.

7. Bernard Leach in Robert Fournier ed., *David Leach: A Potter's Life*, with workshop notes, Fournier Pottery, Lacock, Wilts, second edition, 1979, page 15.

8. David Leach, 'Porcelain Body', *Ceramic Review*, number 2, April, 1970.

9. Emmanuel Cooper, 'An Unassuming Talent', *Ceramic Review*, September/October, number 149, 1994, page 17.

10. Bernard Leach in Robert Fournier ed., *David Leach: A Potter's Life*, with workshop notes, Fournier Pottery, Lacock, Wilts, second edition, 1979, page 6.

11. David Leach, *Crafts* Magazine, May/June, 1979, page 32.

# Chapter Six
# National and International Success

Writing in 1967, David Leach made clear his commitment to achieving an expression of what he called 'one's inmost self', an observation that is particularly relevant not only to his individual pots but to his key role within the potting community. 'The essential difficulties for me', he wrote, 'are always those of discrimination from a truer sensibility out of one's own inmost self, perhaps a self unfitted, too unresolved, too dual a life long search. Is this journey what we mean by the craftsman's way of life?'[1]

While in David's view there is no real distinction between making functional and 'other' pots, for he looks 'on most pots as form', as the tableware became more established his interest turned more and more to the challenge and possibilities of individual pots, which continued to grow in strength and confidence. Keenly aware that the Leach name may be seen as a passport to instant success, he wisely delayed any major exhibitions until he was

David Leach exhibition at the newly opened Cider Press Gallery, Dartington, 1978.

David Leach (right) with (right to Left) Elizabeth Leach, Michael Casson, Sheila Casson, Gallery Upstairs, 1999.

sure that his pots were an expression of his own personality. In the mid-1960s this began to happen and he accepted invitations to show in local and national and then international exhibitions, and his pots were recognised as carrying the stamp of his personality.

His first one-person exhibition in London took place in 1966 at the Craftsmen Potters Shop and Gallery. The exhibition was well-received and in many ways signalled his acclaim as an important individual potter. A year later, when showing pots at the International Academy of Ceramics Exhibition in Istanbul his work was awarded a Gold Medal, confirming that his pots spoke an international language to which others could warmly respond. With growing national and international fame, David was increasingly asked to contribute to mixed shows, and to hold one-person exhibitions in Britain and overseas. Each show saw the further development of previously produced pieces but always with one or two departures, whether with a slight variation in shape, a new glaze or decorative technique.

Writing about David Leach's one-person show in Guildford in 1972, W.A. Ismay the critic and collector, and long-term admirer of David's work, noted 'how clearly as an artist he is able to visualise what he is trying to make', so giving him 'a better-than-average chance of catching the moment of truth'. For Ismay, the 'moment of truth'[2] was that of such formal considerations of line, form, decoration and glaze brought together in a magical combination in which some sort of perfection had been achieved. There was a similar enthusiastic response to David's work from the potter Val Barry when she reviewed a mixed exhibition of porcelain, which included pieces by David. In her view his work had a 'purity of form, an absolute mastery of spatial and linear values and a perfect balance between these and the glaze and decoration'.[3]

The impressive list of David Leach's exhibitions in this country and abroad is a testament to his growing

David Leach lighting his small gas-fired kiln, Lowerdown Pottery, 1994.

David Leach with Clive Bowen who is holding one of David's slipware dishes, 2002.

status among fellow potters, critics and admirers and for what many saw as him moving out of the shadow of his father and establishing himself as a potter in his own right.

As age began to take its toll David produced less tableware preferring to concentrate on individual pieces. With smaller numbers of pots being made, even one chamber of the two-chamber kiln proved too large, and in 1982 he decided that a smaller kiln would be more suitable to his production and duly built a seven cubic foot kiln fired with Propane gas. This could reach temperature in eight hours and, he discovered, could produce results very similar to those obtained in the much slower firings of the large kiln though the body does not 'toast' in the same way. He found that a mixture of finely sieved woodash and gum painted on to the body produced a similar effect. When this small kiln wore out in 2000 he built a new version, and continues to fire it regularly, making pots with the help of his son Jeremy. 'It is better', he commented, 'to fire a small kiln frequently.'[4]

Ever alert to new possibilities, David Leach has recently been involved with a series of collaborations. With Clive Bowen, a potter who lives in north Devon, he has been making press-mould dishes using his original biscuit-fired moulds, and decorating them with trailed slip. These have been fired to earthenware temperature with rich and seductive results. Initially Bowen trained as a potter with David's younger brother Michael, who made high-fired, orientally-inspired stoneware, but he became enamoured of north Devon slipwares. Such forms, which intimately combined form, function and decoration, had also greatly inspired Michael Cardew, who worked at St Ives as Bernard Leach's first apprentice (1923-26). Bowen's strong, sensitive work combines an awareness of and respect for tradition in forms that express a modern sensibility.

Another continuing collaboration is with David Grant at Highland Stoneware, who, in his pottery at Ulapool in Scotland, produces a well-designed range of domestic tableware, made by jiggering and jollying techniques, using a dense white stoneware body. Grant's shapes, often covered with a pale celadon glaze, have a classical simplicity. With David Leach, Grant is developing a jigger and jolly teacup with fluted sides in porcelain based on the shape David Leach has made by hand for many years.

David Leach in his showroom at Lowerdown Pottery standing in front of a photograph of the two chamber oil-fired kiln, packed and ready to fire, Lowerdown Pottery, 1994.

## Ambassadorial and educational involvement

The 'pottery boom' in the late-1950s and 1960s, which saw a huge rise in the number of small studio potters establishing workshops producing functional and decorative wares, led many to think that some sort of association of potters was required, which would serve as a forum for the exchange of information and as a way of possibly marketing their wares. In London there were few specialist outlets, though such large department stores as Liberty and Heal and Sons continued to show studio ceramics as did Primavera in Sloane Street, a shop and gallery set up in 1946 by Henry Rothschild to sell fine craft from this country and abroad.

Amidst great enthusiasm, meetings of potters were arranged, an initial exhibition was set up in London, which proved a great success, and a group of pots were assembled for a show in New Zealand where they sold immediately. In 1958 the Craftsmen Potters Association of Great Britain (now Craft Potters Association of Great Britain) was established as a Friendly Society, as a co-operative to sell the work of its potter members and to increase general awareness of the craft. Rosemary Wren was appointed its first chairman and David Canter, an energetic young businessman, its Honorary Secretary.

Ambitious, resourceful and idealistic, David Canter led the move for the association to find retail premises and establish a shop and gallery in London to sell the work of its members. Premises in Lowndes Court, a narrow lane off Carnaby Street, were acquired on lease and the shop opened in 1960. Initially membership was open to any potter who owned a kiln and ran a studio, but subsequently reservations were expressed about the standard of work shown. Largely because of this Bernard Leach, widely seen as the founding father of the studio pottery movement in Britain and an ideal sponsor, declined to take part but David, hearing about the venture from Colin Pearson, did join and became involved in the enterprise. Enthused by the ideals of the Association and the work it was doing, he became its third chairman in 1967, and went on to serve for many years on the council.

At much the same time David became involved in the setting up of the Devon Guild of Craftsmen in Bovey Tracey in the 1950s, with the aim of presenting the finest work produced in the West Country. The Guild rapidly gained a reputation for showing work of high quality, and David played a key role when it acquired its own premises in the mid-1980s serving as a dedicated and committed chairman. He continues to be closely involved with Guild activities and to offer sound, practical advice.

Having been successful in introducing a deeper understanding of the skills involved in studio pottery to students at Loughborough, David Leach's commitment to a strong practical approach to education was very much in line with the stream of thought within art school education, which believed that courses should be as much skill – as ideas – based. 'Art schools are not so interested in the acquisition of skills as in drawing out the student's creative capacity and ideas, which are sometimes immature and quite unskilfully performed', he argued. 'I think it is important to learn the skills first, then you have the facility to do what you have in your mind successfully.'[5] To students, acquiring skills such as throwing, making up glazes and firing kilns whilst producing attractive functional ware were seen as a way of making a living and David Leach continued to teach part-time at Loughborough until the mid-1960. With his practical and educational experience he was also appointed by the Scottish Education Department as examiner, along with a small team of English potters and educationalists, to look at the Schools of Art in Edinburgh, Glasgow, Dundee and Aberdeen for a three-year period.

One of the most exciting opportunities to influence education came in the early 1960s when the potters Michael Casson and Victor Margrie, who were later to be assisted by Colin Pearson, approached him to discuss the setting up of a two-year vocational course 'Diploma in Studio Pottery' at Harrow School of Art,[6] aimed at teaching particular production skills. David Leach,

David Leach at a workshop visit to Italy, c.1990.

believing that a 'liberal general training' did not make a professional potter, put forward the argument that 'we need more students to accept the slower, radical, disciplined drill of the workshop'[7] and gave the project his full support. He had already been discussing establishing such a course at Loughborough to run alongside the existing three-year course, but it was slow to get going and the proposal from Harrow came along and moved more quickly.

Recognising the growing interest in studio pottery, Casson and Margrie consulted David, and took his advice in planning the course. It was based on the innovatory principle of the atelier system and it would be run largely as a pottery workshop with students directed by practising potters, learning how to produce well-designed and made tableware. In contrast to the more usual ceramics courses, where great emphasis was placed on individual expression, the Harrow course stressed the importance of the acquisition of skill and control before individual style could be developed.[8] Techniques were those of the studio potter such as repetition throwing, involving producing similar shapes from weighted amounts of clay together with some hand-building rather than processes associated with the ceramic industry such as slip-casting or jigger and jollying.

With the support of an enthusiastic college principal the course was set up in 1963 and was immediately oversubscribed for the unique opportunity it offered students to learn to make particular ranges of shapes quickly, efficiently and with a feeling for material. The system was based on that of training apprentices established by David Leach at St Ives, but with a wider variety of teachers and approaches. David's input was greatly valued, and he and

The showroom,
Lowerdown
Pottery, 1994.

Above: Bernard Leach, second from right, visiting Dartington Pottery Training Workshop, Peter Starkey on left, David Leach second from left, David Canter on right. 1976.

Left: David Leach admiring a dish by David Grant, made at Jordanstone College of Art, Dundee, acquired for the George Wenger Collection in Stoke-on-Trent, with Murray Fieldhouse, editor *Pottery Quarterly*, Colin Melbourne and the potter Brian Newman (right).

Helen Pincombe, a potter who had worked for a short time at the Leach Pottery, were appointed as external examiners. The course was seen as a great success leading *Pottery Quarterly*[9] to declare 'Here at last we in Britain have a thorough and practical teutonic [sic] approach to art education'. The magazine was delighted to note that, like the practise of many studio potters, the basis of the course was repetition throwing.

An equally challenging proposal came with the setting up of the Dartington Pottery Training Workshop (DPTW) in 1976. This followed a paper, written by David Leach and the ever-enterprising David Canter, describing their ideas for what they called a 'Community Workshop'. One of its main objectives would be training students to a high standard in workshop production. In 1974 David Canter joined the board of Dartington Hall and obtained permission for the use of a building on the estate as a pottery-training workshop. David Leach and Michael Casson helped plan and implement the scheme, and Dartington Pottery Training Workshop was formed with David Canter as chairman, David Leach, Michael Casson and Marianne de Trey as potter directors. The DPTW was set up in premises alongside those used by Bernard Leach and David in the 1930s when they worked at Dartington.

In one sense, the DPTW grew out of the success of the Diploma in Studio Pottery at Harrow School of Art and the realisation that however thorough the training, the course did not fully equip graduates to set up a workshop, and that some sort of post-graduate experience in a functioning pottery would be useful. Like the Harrow course, the DPTW was also based on the Leach model. It was a chance to put into action an idea developed by David at the Leach Pottery, with pots made for use by a team who did not seek individual recognition and who were willing to refine their skills in a shared workshop. Unlike the Harrow Studio Pottery Course, the DPTW was to be a self-contained training workshop, with a small team of professional potters assisted by trainees producing an established range of reduction-fired tableware. A body of experienced potters was set up to oversee production and a manager appointed.[10]

With funding of £15,000 from the recently set up Crafts Advisory Body[11] (now Crafts Council), and grants for the trainees and no rent to pay to Dartington, the DPTW looked set to become a unique body in serving as

David Leach with the group of students at a workshop, Anderson ranch, Colorado, USA, 1989.

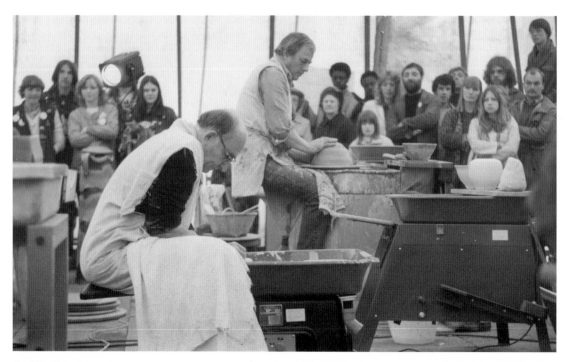

David Leach as guest of honour in foreground demonstrating turning. David Lloyd Jones in background, Northern Potters Jamboree, 1981.

a halfway house for trainees, as well as a pottery in its own right. Bernard Leach paid a visit, and the DPTW received widespread enthusiastic support from potters; the workshop was even made a member of the Craftsmen Potters Association in 1978.[12] Yet, while trainees did acquire invaluable first-hand experience of a working pottery, there were problems with maintaining regular production and without a strong overall image the enterprise had to reconsider its structure in the early 1980s. Eventually the idea of trainees was more or less abandoned, and in 1984 was renamed Dart Pottery (now Dartington Pottery), which, while in many ways continuing to fulfil some of the initial aims of the DPTW, was planned as a more commercial enterprise employing skilled and experienced staff.

The idea of a 'half-way house' where practising potters taught professional pottery skills to both art school graduates and those who showed an aptitude for the craft and who wanted to work as potters, lies at the heart of a new project led by Joe Finch, son of Ray Finch. With his wide experience David Leach has been consulted from the start and is involved in planning discussions, advising and supporting the project. The centre is currently scheduled to be located in south Wales.

David Leach's growing international acclaim as both a distinguished potter and teacher led almost inevitably to being invited to lead workshops in the United States and other countries including Italy, Spain, Norway, Sweden, Holland, Belgium, Venezuela and Germany. Following visits from American potters to Lowerdown Pottery and their enthusiasm for his work, he agreed to spend a month in the States conducting a series of workshops at different venues. His energy, enthusiasm and practical skills made a great impression on his audience. When the American students heard about the Dartington Training Workshop they saw it as fulfilling a much-needed gap and discussed whether such a project could be established in the USA. A group photograph of David Leach at the Anderson Workshop Group, Colorado, confirms the interest of the group. For a workshop in Italy, he wore a t-shirt bearing the slogan 'Old potters never die they just kiln themselves'. It was in many ways typical of his commitment to education and to passing on his skills to others, where he is able to convey a lifetime's experience with humour, goodwill and generosity in an unhesitating belief in the work of the studio potter. David continued to conduct

David Leach
demonstrating at
Inverness, c.1985.

65

David Leach
demonstrating,
USA, c.1985.

workshops until the early 1990s when he decided it was time to hand over to his son Johnnie, who had been holding workshops since the mid-1980s.

## Japan

After leaving Japan in 1920 as a boy of nine, and despite his father's suggestions that he spend a year in the country in the mid-1930s as an alternative to studying in Stoke-on-Trent, David Leach did not return to the country until 1989. The visit was to coincide with a showing of the exhibition St Ives 1939-64, which was mounted at the Tate Gallery, London, in 1985. Four years later the exhibition toured to three major cities in Japan in a slightly reconfigured form that placed the work of his father more at the centre of the show. At the invitation of the Japanese, David Leach was invited to visit Tokyo. Together with the painter Patrick Heron, who, as a conscientious objector, had worked at the Leach Pottery during the war, Oliver Watson, curator of ceramics at the Victoria and Albert Museum and David Brown, a curator at the Tate Gallery, they spoke about Bernard Leach and his work from their first-hand experience. David Leach was able to give an account of his years at the Leach Pottery and offer direct insight into his ideas and working methods.

After a gap of nearly seventy years it was inevitable that David Leach would find the city 'utterly different' with indescribable congestion, whether with 'double-decker' highways in the city or the densely crowded streets. 'When I left in 1920 the city was all single storey buildings now, having solved the earthquake problem, it is quite changed, with sky-scrapers resembling Manhattan,' he comments. Visits were made to Mashiko to see one of Hamada's sons, and to meet Sori Yanagi who was director of the Nihon Mingeikan, the Japanese Folkcraft Museum, and potters who had known his father. Although he was only nine when he left Japan, such buildings as the Imperial Palace with its gardens and moat were remembered, but the vast new developments bore little resemblance to

From left to right: Mrs and Kenji Funaki, David Leach, Mr Shimaoka and Shinsaku Hamada at the Hamada Pottery, Mashiko, Japan, 1989.

David Leach, Teiko Utsumi, curator of the Mingeikan Museum and Sori Yanagi, director of Nihon Mingeikan, Japan, 1989.

David Leach with Sori Yanagi, director of Nihon Mingeikan, Japan, 1989.

David Leach with Kenji Funaki, sharing a workshop. Kenji Funaki was a student at Lowerdown Pottery in 1967.

the city of his childhood. Nevertheless, the visit was a welcome reminder of his time in Japan and, to some extent, of his own pottery roots.

## Potting in the new millennium

At the age of ninety-one and although often intending to 'slow down', David continues to pot as strongly and as sensitively as he ever did, though he now prefers to work a part rather than all day. As a result his output is less prolific but he remains alert to new possibilities, whether in refining a glaze, adapting a shape or in devising new decoration. A constant stream of visitors, anxious to see his work or talk about his life as a potter, ensure that he remains in the thick of things, advising, commenting and giving out information. In an article written in 1992, David Leach described a typical working day as rising at 6.30 and being ready to begin potting at 8.30, working until 1pm when he broke for lunch. When discussing plans for an exhibition he is careful to insist on making a selection that will look well together, 'with a proportion of evolving innovation'.[13] In fact the working day varies little from that of sixty years ago.

Even in old age he still relishes the challenge of making a teapot that pours well, has a well-fitting lid and looks good. Occasionally he will make small items of tableware if required to fill a kiln, and help his son Jeremy prepare in the Gilbert dough mixer a ton of clay over a two-day period to be stored to age and mature, but most of the time he is drawn to making individual pots. Ever alert to different ideas, whether in finding ways of making large bottles or collaborating with other potters, he retains a broad interest in pots and what other potters are doing. Porcelain continues to be the material with which he feels most at ease, saying that as a 'more precise potter ...I am led towards porcelain which is rather demanding in these terms. Stoneware needs to be broader and stronger – this is not my nature particularly.'[14] Nevertheless, there is strength and conviction in his stoneware, which has its own characteristics.

David Leach's is a true exploration and celebration of the 'craftsman's way of life', both for the integrity of the making, his involvement in the wider concerns of potters and his determination to evolve his own voice within a tradition shaped by his father. At the age of ninety-one he has been making pots for

David Leach in front of Lowerdown Pottery, 1994.

A group of biscuit fired bottles fresh from the kiln waiting to be glazed, height about 350mm, Lowerdown Pottery, 2002.

David Leach, stoneware and porcelain pots ready for sorting for exhibition, Lowerdown Pottery, 1997.

over seventy years, half of which has been as an independent potter, moving from the role of skilled and able manager to an independent individual artist potter. When he was awarded the OBE in 1987 it was not only for his remarkable achievements as a potter but also in recognition of his contribution to a wider understanding of the art and craft of pottery, whether through education, involvement in organisations such as the Craft Potters Association and the Devon Guild of Craftsmen, or through his ambassadorial role in advocating the qualities of the craft.

When writing about David's ceramics in 1977, his father, then an old man of ninety, spoke of his son's search for truth, 'in the broad sense of what any work should be – what the relationship to beauty and art is',[15] and few would deny this as a crucial part of David Leach's work. In the same year David wrote that 'when one grows older one learns to accept oneself, warts and all', adding 'the pot must be an expression of the man'. Twenty-five years later it is his pots that stand as his finest and most enduring achievement, and these are testament to a full, rich and generous life.

David and Elizabeth Leach in their garden at Lowerdown Cross.

**FOOTNOTES**

1. *Pottery Quarterly: A Review of Ceramic Art* vol. 9, no 33. (1967).

2. W. A. Ismay, David Leach, Guildford, 1972, *Ceramic Review*, July/August, number 16, 1972.

3. Val Barry, 'Porcelain: Craftsmen Potters Shop, London, April, 1973', *Ceramic Review*, July/August, number 24, 1973.

4. David Leach, 'A Potter's Day', *Ceramic Review*, November/December, number 138, 1992.

5. David Leach, 'Good for a thousand years', *For a Change*, vol. 14, no. 2, April/May 2001, p. 8.

6. Now the University of Westminster.

7. Tanya Harrod, *The Crafts in Britain in the 20th Century*, Yale University Press, New Haven and London, 1999, p. 240.

8. The practical expectations of the students on the course were graphically illustrated when in response to the need to write a thesis, one student took the title 'Why are we being asked to write a thesis', claiming that she had come to learn practical pottery skills rather than acquire a literary education.

9. 'Harrow School of Art', *Pottery Quarterly: A Review of Ceramic Art*, vol. 8, no. 32.

10. In addition to the governing board, Colin Kellam, Geoffrey Whiting and John Maltby were active supporters. The manager was Peter Starkey.

11. David Leach had served as a member of the Grants Committee after the CAC was first set up in 1973.

12. For a full account of the DPTW in operation see Murray Fieldhouse 'The Dartington Pottery Training Workshop', *Ceramic Review*, July/August, number 58, 1979.

13. David Leach, 'A Potter's Day', *Ceramic Review*, November/December, number 138, 1992.

14. David Leach in Robert Fournier ed. *David Leach: A Potter's Life*, with workshop notes, Fournier Pottery, Lacock, Wilts, second edition, 1979, page 16.

15. Bernard Leach in Fournier, page 6.

# David Leach – 20th Century Ceramics

This exhibition of 130 pots takes the reader on a lifetime's journey – David Leach's life as a potter since 1930. We have pots from each decade including those made at the last possible date before final selection in October 2002. Happily, his latest endeavour in his long-standing interest in uniting the practical aspects of industrial production with handcrafted pottery bore fruit 'just in time' with the project to make the Y-Ching glazed, fluted porcelain tea set in conjunction with Highland Stoneware of Lochinver, Scotland (*exhibits 58 and 59*).

David Leach has been committed to pottery since 1930 and has always shared his knowledge and love of the subject as widely as possible. He delayed an independent career as a potter because he believed that he had something useful to contribute to his father's pottery at St Ives. He rescued the Leach Pottery by attending the Pottery Managers' Training Course in Stoke-on-Trent and changing working practices on his return. He saw the value of a Standard range of tableware, available through retailers, mail order and direct sales. On setting up Lowerdown Pottery in 1956 he grasped the challenge of designing pots in his own style and making them to exacting specifications.

The exhibition is based on three main themes:
1. Pots and potters who have been an inspiration to David throughout his lifetime, since he began potting more than 70 years ago.
2. Pots which David and his co-workers have made at the Leach Pottery, St Ives; Aylesford Priory, Kent; Lowerdown Pottery, Bovey Tracey, Devon and during lecture/demonstration events.
3. Pots made by four apprentices and students from among the many who have benefited from working at Lowerdown Pottery.

## Pots and potters who have inspired David Leach

David Leach readily acknowledges his debt to his father Bernard Leach, who was one of the pioneers of studio pottery in Britain. He felt it very important to include the iconic *Leaping Salmon* vase as a tribute to his mentor (*exhibit 1*). He remembers Michael Cardew, the first student at the Leach Pottery, 1923-1926, and has enjoyed owning this slipware jug (*exhibit 2*). In spite of its fragility David insisted that the pot be shown in the exhibition as a mark of his great respect for an outstanding twentieth-century potter.

Ideas for shapes and patterns have been inspired by other cultures. Chinese ceramics of the Song Dynasty (*Northern Song 960-1127, Southern Song 1128-1279*) have had a profound influence upon David Leach's personal work. He found the quality of glazes especially important in the development of his own style – celadon including Y-Ching, that special pale blue described as 'sky after rain', temmoku and crackle (Guan ware). In his portfolio of decoration he has made fluting, engraving and painting special features, as did his Chinese predecessors (*see section of individual artistic pots*). Two of David's bowls in this exhibition are based on diverse themes – patterns on blankets designed by Navajo Indians (*exhibit 4*) and an early bowl made either in Crete or Cyprus. His first bowl in this style was made in 1946 and has been lost, but in 2001 he remade it (*exhibit 3*).

David Leach respects the quality of Richard Batterham's work. He has impressed David by his complete dedication to the craftsman's life, rather than assuming an artist's stance and the fact that he has always worked alone (*exhibit 5*). David's eldest son John is included in this section because David admires the success of the Muchelney Pottery domestic range. John's tall jug is robust and the strength of the throwing is so clear (*exhibit 7*) and the elements which make up his cross-handle bottle blend so successfully *(exhibit 8)*. In spite of its tiny stature, David feels that the cream jug, made for so many years by Nick Rees at Muchelney, has integrity, as seen in the way in which the rim, the beautiful toasted exterior and the glaze work together *(exhibit 6)*.

# Pots made by David Leach from 1930

### Pots made at Dartington Hall, Devon and the Leach Pottery, St Ives, Cornwall, 1930-1955

Naturally enough David's red earthenware vessels are influenced by pots made by Bernard Leach and Michael Cardew, two of the most significant pioneers of handmade pottery in Britain and we are fortunate to have pots made during this very early period, 1930-1937. Remarkably the burnished globular pot *(exhibit 11)*, made at Dartington in 1934 was refired in 2001, resulting in the dual colours, red earthenware and black smoked surface. The magnificent slipware charger with pagoda design *(exhibit 13)* was a deliberate attempt by David to echo his father's work.

I am grateful to be able to include what might be considered an unimportant little plate *(exhibit 14)*. Collected by the scholar, Dr Henry Bergen, this stoneware plate was made in 1937 at the Leach Pottery under the new regime implemented by David on his return from studying on the Pottery Managers' Course in Stoke-on-Trent. It marks the change from earthenware to stoneware production and the beginning of the revival of the Leach Pottery. As was usual, no personal identification is impressed in this plate but David confirmed its origin during a visit to The Potteries Museum & Art Gallery, Stoke-on-Trent in 1982.

By the early 1950s David had developed a porcelain body which was light and highly translucent, it threw well and could be gracefully fluted. The teacup and saucer *(exhibit 15)* was a trial for the now well known and admired Y-Ching tea sets. David believes that it excels all the others he made, because later he was obliged to change the ingredients of the porcelain body. I suspect that this is the opinion of the perfectionist since so many people are delighted to be the owners of David's fluted Y-Ching glazed tea ware and bowls.

The mead set, commissioned by Francis Fawcett a mead maker of High Wycombe, was designed and made by David Leach in 1949 *(exhibit 17)*. The mead set and the dinner plate with engraved oak leaf under celadon glaze *(exhibit 18)* give an insight into the high quality of the Leach Pottery Standard range which was made for more than a quarter of a century. Original ideas for items to be included in the range came from both Bernard and David, with David developing the shapes sketched by his father from first models to successful completion.

### Pots made at Lowerdown Pottery, Bovey Tracey, Devon from 1956

David's first five years at Lowerdown, 1956-61, saw the production of slipware and tin-glazed earthenware. Both are based on red earthenware clay but finished with entirely different glazes.

### Slipware

Slipware pottery has a long tradition in Britain and has been in continuous production somewhere in the country since the seventeenth century. The basic pot is made in red earthenware clay which is covered with white slip (liquid clay), and decorated in a contrasting coloured clay by trailing a fine line of slip over the surface *(exhibits 21 and 26)*. Sometimes a design is scratched from the slip layer, revealing the red clay body – a method called sgraffito. David used a green glaze on some pots *(exhibits 22 and 23)*.

David has enjoyed making slipware throughout his career and as recently as November 2001 shared a kiln with Clive Bowen, an accomplished slipware potter from Shebbear in North Devon. Whilst working together at a demonstration in Bideford they fired ten large oval dishes. Each was impressed with both potters' marks – a unique and successful collaboration (*exhibits 27 and 28*).

## Tin-glaze

Tin-glaze made at Lowerdown Pottery by David Leach varies greatly from the tin-glaze made by European potters from the fifteenth century onwards. Its predominant colour is white – the glaze is made white and opaque by the addition of tin oxide and patterns are painted on to this unfired, powdery glaze surface. The glaze and decoration are fired together, the colour sinking into the surface of the tin-glaze.

David's tin-glaze is predominantly greyish in colour with white highlights. The red earthenware body was covered with slip which had been stained brown with manganese and iron, before receiving its coat of white tin-glaze. The combination of the brown slip and the white tin-glaze resulted in an overall greyish hue. Patterns were cut through the glaze layer into the brown slip layer and the white tin-glaze gathered in the resultant grooves. On a few occasions, spots of green glaze were added for a different effect (*exhibits 30 and 34*).

## Pots made at Lowerdown Pottery 1961 onwards

David Leach's mature style emerged as the result of building his big kiln in 1961. This two-chambered kiln, built on oriental principles, was fired by wood and oil to very high temperatures. From time to time during the firing cycle, the amount of oxygen in the kiln atmosphere was reduced. It was during this 'reduction' period that marvellous effects in glazes and decoration took place.

Using this kiln David was able to make his tableware and individual pots in stoneware and porcelain clays and during the last half century his work has shown consistency in both shape and decorative motif. He has preferred to work within known parameters aiming to make high quality pots and he has not allowed himself to be seduced by fashion and short-lived fads. The resulting body of work stands as a tribute to his technical and design skills.

| Shapes | Exhibit Numbers |
|---|---|
| tall bottle vases | 81, 82, 106, 107, 108 |
| robust jars | 77, 78, 89, 103, 104, 105 |
| chargers | 96 |
| fluted bowls | 67-76 |
| delicate lidded boxes | 83-88 |
| miniature bottle vases | 109-118 |
| tableware stoneware | 39-57 |
| tableware porcelain | 58-66 |

| Glazes | Exhibit Numbers |
|---|---|
| celadon | 42, 49, 50, 56, 57, 61, 80, 81, 87, 111 |
| David's yellow celadon | 67, 73 |
| Y-Ching | 58, 59, 60, 68 |
| temmoku | 41, 44, 51, 71, 77, 90, 98, 104, 105, 106 |
| crackle | 65, 84, 101, 117, 118 |
| dolomite | 47, 48, 79, 92, 96, 97, 103, 108, 116 |
| gun metal | 66, 75, 110 |
| reduced copper red/ox-blood | 69, 70 |
| oatmeal | 52, 78 |
| chun | 76 |
| ash | 91, 107 |
| titanium | 55 |

| Motifs | Exhibit Numbers |
|---|---|
| foxglove | 46-50, 62, 63, 102-105 |
| willow tree | 77-83 |
| zigzag | 106, 107, 108 |
| waves | 85, 86, 94, 95, 96 |
| floral cluster | 40, 92, 93 |

| Method of decoration | Exhibit Numbers |
|---|---|
| painted | 39, 43, 45, 46, 53, 54, 62, 63, 64, 80, 81, 83, 88, 89, 93, 94, 95, 99, 100, 102, 104, 105, 106, 112-114 |
| wax resist | 79, 92, 96, 97, 103, 108 |
| sgraffito | 98 |
| fluting | 41, 42, 58, 60, 61, 67-76, 87 |
| engraved | 55, 82 |
| combed | 77, 78, 107 |
| colour wash background | 64, 86, 88, 89 |

# Apprentices and students at Lowerdown Pottery

David Leach has been an excellent, sensitive and generous teacher. Many apprentices have been trained at Lowerdown, moving on to make successful careers as independent potters. Numerous student potters have spent time at Lowerdown and benefited from working with David. Sadly we have been unable to identify any pots made by the first Lowerdown apprentice, Freda Sage (1957-1961), but we suspect that her hand may have touched some of the early Lowerdown pots included in the exhibition.

Four established potters were invited to represent the many Lowerdown apprentices and students in David's celebratory exhibition. Their work is individual and has no likeness to David's. Each gained from a grounding which has 'stood them in good stead' as can be seen by the originality of their work.

### John Leach, Muchelney Pottery, Muchelney, Somerset since 1964
David's eldest son, working at Lowerdown 1957-1960
Black Mood pots, stoneware, fired in saggars with sawdust which burns and deposits carbon on their surfaces *(exhibits 119, 120, 121)*

### John Maltby, The Orchard House, Stoneshill, Crediton, Devon since 1963
Apprentice 1960-1963
Figures, stoneware, modelled, painted details *(exhibits 122, 123, 124)*.

### Tim Andrews, Woodbury Pottery, Woodbury, Exeter, Devon since 1993
Apprentice 1978-1979, further training at Dartington Pottery Training Workshop 1979-1981, returned as fully fledged, independent potter to share the workshop and kiln with David 1986-1993
Forms, raku fired, burnished glazes *(exhibits 125, 126, 127)*.

### Elizabeth Raeburn, Pilltown Chapel, West Pennard, near Glastonbury, Somerset since 1975
Student placement of six to eight weeks, during summer holiday between years one and two of the Harrow Pottery course, 1974.
Forms, raku fired, burnished glazes *(exhibits 128, 129, 130)*.

Kathy Niblett
Exhibition Curator
© 2002

# Pots and potters who have inspired David Leach

## Numbers 1-8

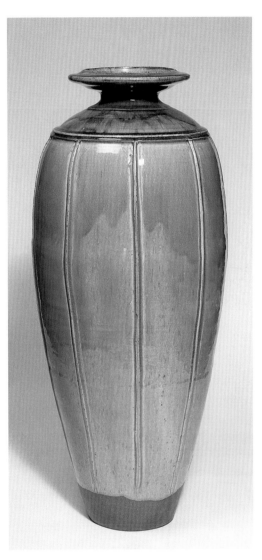

**1**
**Vase**, Leaping Salmon, stoneware, made by Bernard Leach, the Leach Pottery, St Ives, 1931, h.327mm. Dean Milner-White Collection. *Kindly loaned by York Museums Trust (York Art Gallery).*

**5**
**Bottle vase**, stoneware, celadon glaze, cobalt on shoulder and neck, made by Richard Batterham, Durweston, Dorset, 2002, h.810mm. *Kindly loaned by Richard Batterham.*

**2**
**Jug**, red earthenware clay, slipware, made by Michael Cardew, Winchcombe Pottery, Gloucestershire, 1930s, h.255mm.

**4**
**Bowl**, stoneware, sgraffito pattern through black slip layer, celadon glaze inside, made by David Leach, Lowerdown Pottery, Devon, 1985 d.299mm. Pattern inspired by decorative motifs of Navajo Indians.

**3**
**Bowl**, stoneware, sgraffito lines through temmoku glaze, made by David Leach, Lowerdown Pottery, Devon, 2001, d.230mm. Based on an original bowl in the Victoria and Albert Museum, London, from Crete or Cyprus.

**6**
**Cream jug**, wood-fired stoneware, made at Muchelney Pottery, Somerset, 2002, h.96mm.
**7**
**Jug**, wood-fired stoneware, made by John Leach, Muchelney Pottery, Somerset, 2002, h.432mm.
**8**
**Cross handle bottle**, ash glaze, wood-fired stoneware, made by John Leach, Muchelney Pottery, Somerset, 1996, h.140mm.

*Kindly loaned by John Leach.*

# Pots made by David Leach at Dartington Hall, Devon and the Leach Pottery, St Ives, Cornwall

Numbers 9-18

Numbers 16 and 18 made by unidentified assistant potters

**13**
**Dish**, slipware, made at the Leach Pottery, St Ives, about 1935, d.326mm. After a Bernard Leach design.

**9**
**Vase**, slipware, D seal mark, made at Dartington Hall, Devon, 1933, h.229mm.

**10**
**Vase**, slipware, impressed D in a circle, made at Dartington Hall, Devon, 1933, h.210mm. Dartington Hall Trust Collection. *Kindly loaned by Dartington Hall Trust.*

**11**
**Vase**, red earthenware clay, burnished, incised D, made at Dartington Hall, Devon, 1934, h.159mm.

**12**
**Jug**, slipware, impressed SI, made at the Leach Pottery, St Ives, dated 1935, h.255mm.

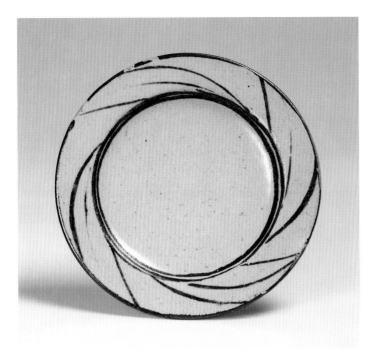

**15**
**Tea cup and saucer**, translucent porcelain, fluted, Y-Ching glaze, the original design, made at the Leach Pottery, St Ives, early 1950s, h. cup 64mm.

**14**
**Plate**, stoneware, painted, impressed SI, made at the Leach Pottery, St Ives, 1937, d.176mm. Dr Henry Bergen Collection. *Kindly loaned by The Potteries Museum & Art Gallery, Stoke-on-Trent.*

**16**
**Tankard**, stoneware, ash glaze over iron slip, impressed SI, made at the Leach Pottery, St Ives, early 1950s, h.110mm.

**18**
**Plate**, stoneware, Leach Standard Ware, engraved oak leaf, celadon glaze, made at the Leach Pottery, St Ives, 1946-1955, d.248mm.

**17**
**Mead set**, stoneware, celadon glaze, raised letters on a pad of clay F.F.MEAD, impressed SI, made at the Leach Pottery, St Ives, 1949, h. carafe 189mm, h. goblet 64mm.

# Slipware made by David Leach 1954-2001

Numbers 19-28

**20**
**Casserole dish** and lid, red earthenware, covered with black slip glaze, made at Lowerdown Pottery, Devon, 1956-1961, d.280mm.

**19**
**Dish**, slipware, press moulded, impressed DL AP, made at Aylesford Priory, Kent, 1954, length 413mm.

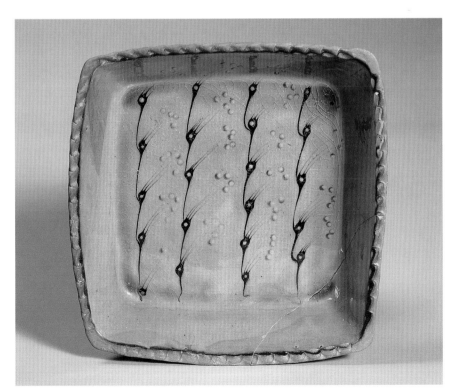

**21**
**Dish**, slipware, press moulded, slip trailed in brown, yellow glaze, made at Lowerdown Pottery, Devon, 1956-1961, w.255mm.

**22**
**Vase**, slipware, white slip layer, slip trailed in brown, green glaze, made at Lowerdown Pottery, Devon, 1956-1961, h.229mm.

**23**
**Cider jar**, slipware, white slip layer, slip trailed in white, combed decoration, green glaze, made at Lowerdown Pottery, Devon, 1956-1961, h.229mm.

**24**
**Jug**, slipware, slip trailed in brown, made at Lowerdown Pottery, Devon, 1956-1961, h.255mm.

**25**
**Jug**, red earthenware, covered with black slip glaze, slip trailed in brown and white, *one & all*, made at Lowerdown Pottery, Devon, 1956-1961, h.261mm.

**26**
**Dish**, slipware, press moulded, slip trailed in brown, yellow glaze, made in Germany, 1993, d.350mm.

**27**
**Dish**, slipware, press moulded, slip trailed in brown, yellow glaze, made with Clive Bowen at Bideford, Devon, impressed CB DL, 2001, length 451mm.

**28**
**Dish**, slipware, press moulded, slip trailed, yellow glaze with green overtones, made with Clive Bowen at Bideford, Devon, impressed CB DL, 2001, length 432mm.

# Tin-glaze, made by David Leach at Lowerdown Pottery, Devon 1956-1961

Numbers 29-38

Numbers 32 and 33 made by unidentified assistant potters

David Leach's tin-glaze – red earthenware clay body is covered with a slip stained brown with manganese and iron before being coated with white tin-glaze. Patterns were cut through (sgraffito) the glaze layer and the finished effect is of a greyish glaze with a white pattern. This resulted when the white tin-glaze collected in the cuts and so remained white.

**29**
**Vase**, tin-glazed earthenware, c.1958, h.240mm.

**30**
**Plate**, tin-glazed earthenware, ears of corn, spots of green glaze,1956-1961, d.248mm.

**31**
**Plate**, tin-glazed earthenware, bamboo design, 1956-1961, d.134mm.

**32**
**Butter dish and lid**, tin-glazed earthenware, abstract pattern, 1956-1961, d.147mm.

**37**
**Jam pot and lid**, tin-glazed earthenware, 1956-1961, h.102mm.

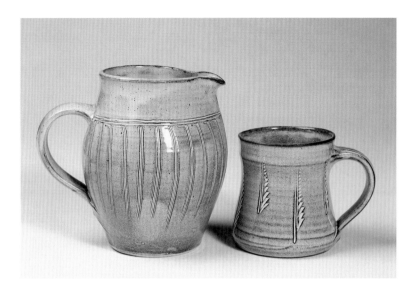

**35**
**Jug**, tin-glazed earthenware, engraved, 1956-1961, h.140mm.

**36**
**Mug**, tin-glazed earthenware, ears of corn, 1956-1961, h.89mm.

**34**
**Jug**, tin-glazed earthenware, green glaze on rim and handle, 1956-1961, h.172mm.

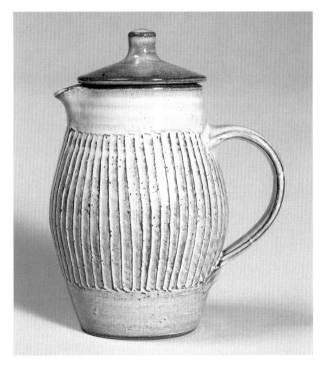

**38**
**Oil and vinegar bottles**, tin-glazed earthenware, scrolls and names, 1956-1961, h.121mm.

**33**
**Jug and lid**, tin-glazed earthenware, fluted, 1956-1961, h.178mm.

# Tableware, made by David Leach in stoneware clay at Lowerdown Pottery, Devon, since 1961

Numbers 39-57

Numbers 44-50, 52, 55-57 made by unidentified assistant potters

**39**
**Teapot**, stoneware, painted with blue dashes, 1961, h.102mm.

**40**
**Teapot**, stoneware, painted with stylised floral motif, trailed spots in iron red, 1961, h.102mm.

**42**
**Teapot**, stoneware, fine fluting, pulled handle, celadon glaze, c.1995, h.150mm.

**43**
**Teapot**, stoneware, painted in blue and brown, trailed spots in brown, c.1994, h.166mm.

**41**
**Teapot**, stoneware, fluted, temmoku glaze, c.1990, h.166mm.
*Kindly loaned by The Rudolf Strasser Collection, Munich.*

**46**
**General Purpose bowl and individual bowl**, stoneware, painted foxglove, 1966, GP bowl d.255mm, bowl d.144mm.

47          49          48          50

**Mugs made from 1965**,
from left to right
**47**
**Mug**, stoneware, dolomite glaze, painted foxglove, h.83mm.

**49**
**Tankard**, stoneware, celadon glaze, painted foxglove, h.121mm.

**48**
**Mug**, stoneware, dolomite glaze, painted foxglove, h.89mm.

**50**
**Mug**, stoneware, flared mouth, celadon glaze, painted foxglove, h.102mm.

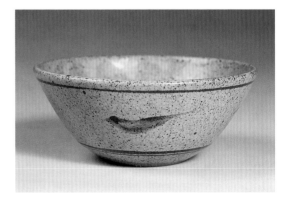

**45**
**Individual bowl**, stoneware, painted, d.147mm, c.1975.

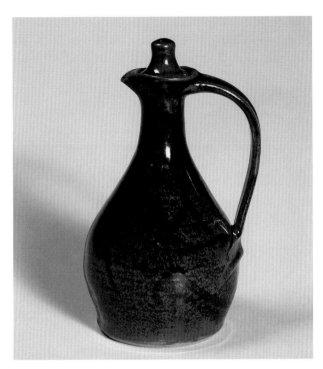

**52**
**Cream jug**, stoneware, iron slip under oatmeal glaze which has cracked like ice outside, oatmeal glaze inside, h.123mm.

**51**
**Oil or vinegar bottle**, stoneware, temmoku glaze, h.153mm. The pair would be in celadon glaze.

**53**
**Tray**, stoneware, press moulded, speckled dolomite glaze, painted, fly ash glaze on back, length 153mm.

**54**
**Dish**, stoneware, speckled dolomite glaze, painted, trailed spots in iron red, d.121mm.

**44**
**Coffee set**, stoneware, temmoku glaze inside, fly ash glaze outside, coffee pot h.134mm, mug h.70mm, c.1975.

**55**
**Dish**, stoneware, carved, titanium glaze, 1975-1980, d.110mm.

**56**
**Casserole and lid**, stoneware, celadon glaze inside, fly ash glaze outside, d.229mm.

**57**
**Individual bowls**, stoneware, celadon glaze inside, unglazed outside, d.145mm, d.110mm.

# Tea ware, made by David Leach in porcelain clay at Lowerdown Pottery, Devon, since 1961

## Numbers 58-66

**58**
**Tea set**, porcelain, fluted, Y-Ching glaze, teapot h.166mm, creamer h.107mm, saucer d.141mm, cup h.66mm, c.1995.

**59**
**Tea set**, porcelain, fluted, Y-Ching glaze, tea cup, saucer and sugar bowl made by semi-automatic methods, teapot and creamer made by hand at Highland Stoneware Pottery, Lochinver, Scotland, 2002, tea pot h. 170mm. *Kindly loaned by David Grant, Highland Stoneware Limited.*

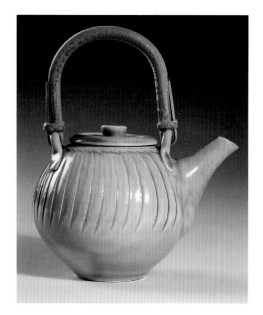

**63**
**Tea jar and lid**, porcelain, painted, trailed iron red spots, foxglove, late 1980s, h.121mm.

**61**
**Teapot and lid**, porcelain, fluted, celadon glaze, h.102mm, c.1985.

**62**
**Teapot and lid**, porcelain, painted, trailed iron red spots, foxglove, 1970s, h.146mm.

**60**
**Tea jar and lid**, porcelain, fluted, pale celadon glaze, 2002, h.96mm.

**64**
**Tea jar and lid**, porcelain, painted blue wash background, painted, trailed iron red spots, 1977, h.127mm.

**66**
**Coffee set**, porcelain, thrown, profile tool used to create raised lines, gun metal glaze, coffee pot h.178mm, jug h.89mm, cup h.57mm.

**65**
**Teapot and lid**, porcelain, matt white dolomite glaze, crackle in glaze stained pink, 1981, h.97mm. *Kindly loaned by The Potteries Museum & Art Gallery, Stoke-on-Trent.*

# Individual artistic pots made by David Leach at Lowerdown Pottery, Devon since 1961

### Numbers 67-118

**67**
**Bowl**, porcelain, fluted, yellow celadon glaze, 2002, d.153mm.

**69**
**Bowl**, porcelain, fluted, reduced copper red glaze, d.189mm.

**68**
**Bowl**, fluted, Y-Ching, celadon 'sky after rain' glaze, 1995, d.134mm.

**70**
**Tea bowl** (centre), porcelain, fluted, reduced copper red glaze, 1985, d.106mm.

**71**
**Bowl** (left), porcelain, fluted, temmoku glaze, 1981, d.133mm.

**72**
**Bowl** (right), porcelain, fluted, matt dolomite glaze with iron speckles, d.117mm.

Ballantyne Collection.
*Kindly loaned by Castle Museum, Nottingham.*

**73**
**Bowl,** porcelain, fluted, yellow celadon glaze,
2002, h.128mm.

**76**
**Bowl**, stoneware, fluted, temmoku glaze breaking to pale blue chun glaze, 1988, h.102mm.

**74**
**Bowl,** stoneware, fluted, matt
dolomite glaze, 1990,
h.123mm.

**75**
**Bowl**, stoneware, fluted, gun
metal glaze, 1990, h.102mm.

**77**
**Jar**, stoneware, tall, combed decoration through temmoku glaze, stylised willow tree, 1966, h.610mm. One of the pots shown at David Leach's first solo exhibition at the Craftsmen Potters Association (now the Craft Potters Association), London, 1966.

**78**
**Jar**, stoneware, combed decoration through oatmeal glaze over iron slip, stylised willow tree, 1970s, h.230mm.

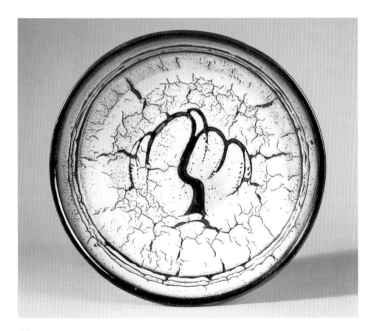

**79**
**Dish**, stoneware, wax resist willow tree, dolomite over temmoku glaze, 1991, d.356mm.

**82**
**Bottle vase**, porcelain, engraved willow tree, grey glaze, h.280mm, c.1990.

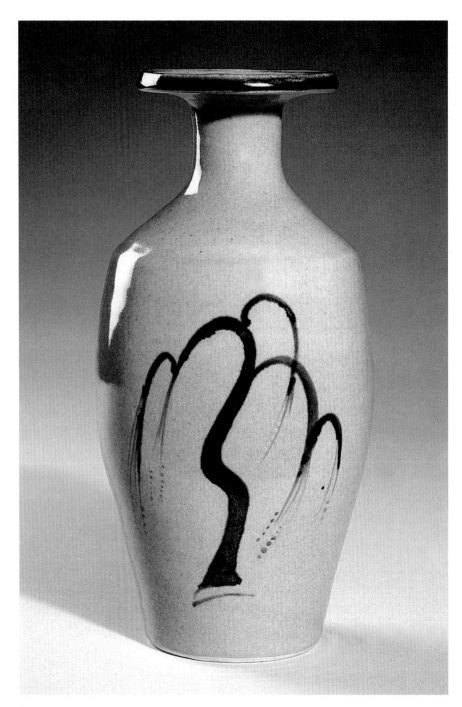

**81**
**Bottle vase**, porcelain, painted willow tree with trailed iron red spots, celadon glaze, 1989, h.292mm.

**83**
**Box and lid** (centre), porcelain, painted
willow tree with trailed iron red spots, 1991,
d.110mm.

**84**
**Box and lid** (left), porcelain, matt white
dolomite glaze, crackle in glaze stained pink,
1980, d.110mm.

**85**
**Box and lid** (right), porcelain, painted
waves motif with trailed iron red spots,
1990, d.110mm.

**86**
**Box and lid**, porcelain, painted blue
wash background, painted waves motif
with trailed iron red spots, 1981,
d.112mm.

**87**
**Box and lid**, porcelain, fluted, celadon
glaze, 1981, d.95mm.

**88**
**Box and lid**, stoneware, painted blue
wash background, painted floral motif
with trailed iron red spots, d.100mm.

Ballantyne Collection. *Kindly loaned by
Castle Museum, Nottingham.*

**80**
**Bud vase**, stoneware, painted willow tree with trailed
iron red spots, celadon glaze, h.180mm, c.1995.

**89**
**Jar**, stoneware, painted blue wash background, painted floral motif with trailed iron red spots, h.240mm, c.1985.

**90**
**Bottle vase**, stoneware, indented, temmoku glaze, c.2000, h.288mm.

**92**
**Bottle vase**, stoneware, wax resist floral motif, dolomite over temmoku glaze, 2002, h.330mm.

**91**
**Cider jar**, stoneware, cross handle, grey mottled ash glaze over iron slip, early 1960s, h.482mm.

**93**
**Bowl** (right) , porcelain, matt white dolomite glaze, painted floral motif, c.2000, d.178mm.

**94**
**Bowl** (left), porcelain, painted waves motif with trailed brown spots, c.1980, d.153mm.

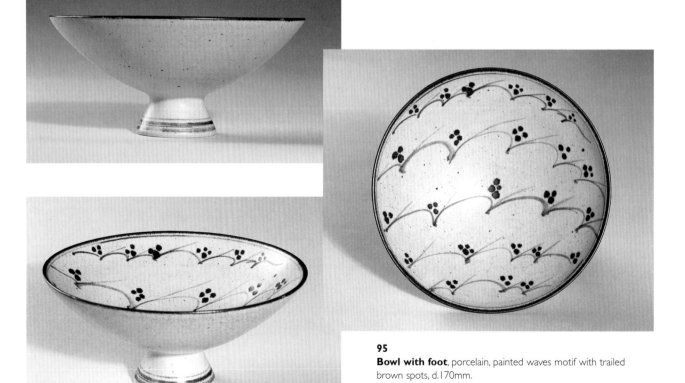

**95**
**Bowl with foot**, porcelain, painted waves motif with trailed brown spots, d.170mm.

**97**
**Bowl**, stoneware, wax resist, dolomite over
temmoku glaze, 1977 d.413mm. Bought
from the opening exhibition at the Cider
Press Gallery, Dartington, 1977, which was a
solo exhibition of pots by David Leach. See
photograph page 57.

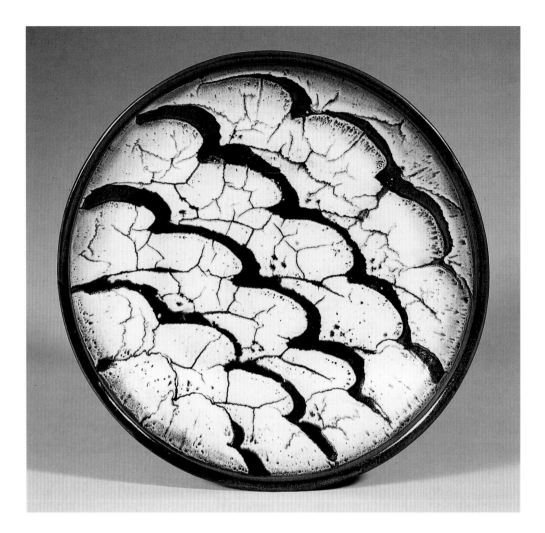

**96**
**Charger**, stoneware, wax resist waves motif, dolomite over temmoku glaze, 1995, d.368mm.

**98**
**Bowl**, porcelain, sgraffito through light temmoku glaze, d.217mm, c.1980.

**99**
**Bowl**, porcelain, matt white dolomite glaze, painted lines and red spots, 2002, d.153mm.

**100**
**Bowl**, porcelain, matt white dolomite glaze, painted Z motif, 1990, d.121mm.
A characteristic motif from the Leach Pottery, St Ives.

**102**
**Bowl**, porcelain, matt white dolomite glaze, painted foxglove motif and trailed iron red spots, 1976, d.159mm.

**101**
**Vase**, porcelain, thrown and blown, matt white dolomite glaze, crackle in glaze stained pink, 1983, h.102mm.

**103**
**Jar**, stoneware, wax resist foxglove motif, dolomite over temmoku glaze, 1995, h.191mm.

**105**
**Jar** (below), stoneware, squat, painted foxglove motif in ilmenite over temmoku glaze, 1984, h.300mm.

**104**
**Jar** (above), stoneware, tall, painted foxglove motif in ilmenite over temmoku glaze, 1977, h.425mm. Bought from the opening exhibition at the new Cider Press Gallery, Dartington, 1977, which was a solo exhibition of pots by David Leach. Dartington Hall Trust Collection. *Kindly loaned by Dartington Hall Trust.*

**106**
**Bottle vase**,
stoneware, painted
zigzag motif in ilmenite
over temmoku glaze,
1982, h.508mm.

**107**
**Bottle vase**,
stoneware, combed
zigzag motif, ash glaze
over iron slip, h.534mm,
1990.

**108**
**Bottle vase**, stoneware, wax
resist zigzag motif, dolomite
over temmoku glaze, 1996,
h.395mm.

**A collection of miniature bottles made at
Lowerdown Pottery in the 1990s**

**109**
Stoneware, facetted,
dolomite over temmoku
glaze, 2002, h.89mm.

**110**
Stoneware, facetted, gun
metal glaze, h.83mm.

**111**
Stoneware, flattened sides,
celadon glaze, h.100mm.

**112**
Stoneware, painted in blue,
trailed iron red spots, 2002,
h.88mm.

**113**
Stoneware, painted in blue
and brown, trailed iron red
spots, h.90mm.

**114**
Stoneware, painted brown
and blue lines, h.63mm.

**115**
Porcelain, facetted, matt
white glaze with brown iron
spots, h.65mm.

**116**
Porcelain, round vertical
sides, matt white dolomite
glaze, h.88mm.

**117**
Porcelain, flattened sides,
matt white dolomite glaze,
crackle in glaze stained pink,
h.90mm.

**118**
Porcelain, off-set facets,
matt white dolomite glaze,
crackle in glaze stained pink,
1981, h.83mm.

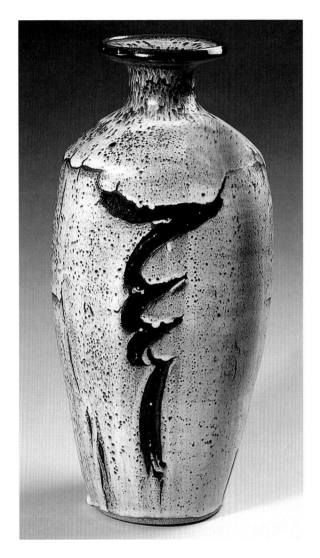

# Recent work from a few of the apprentices and students who worked at Lowerdown Pottery

**John Leach – Black Mood**
**119**
**Sack pot**, stoneware, saggar fired, made by John Leach, Muchelney, Somerset, 2002, h.165mm.

**120**
**Shallow dish**, stoneware, saggar fired, made by John Leach, Muchelney, Somerset, 2002, d.153mm.

**121**
**Lug vase**, stoneware, saggar fired, made by John Leach, Muchelney, Somerset, 2002, h.165mm.

*Kindly loaned by John Leach.*

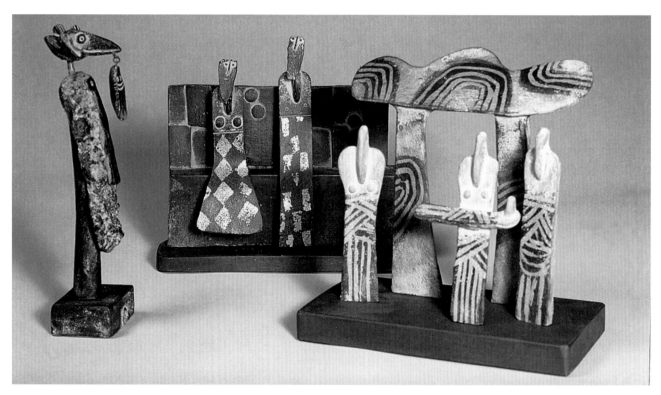

**John Maltby**
**122**
**Fisherman and bird**, stoneware, made by John Maltby, Crediton, Devon, 2002, h.280mm.

*Kindly loaned by Roundhouse Gallery, Foston, Derbyshire.*

**123**
**King and Queen**, stoneware, painted with gold, made by John Maltby, Crediton, Devon, 2002, h.248mm.

**124**
**Three figures in a wood**, stoneware, made by John Maltby, Crediton, Devon, 2002, h.261mm.

**Tim Andrews**
**125**
**Humbug**, raku, black and white resist, made by Tim Andrews, Woodbury, Exeter, Devon, 2002, d.290mm.

**126**
**Form**, raku, black and white resist, made by Tim Andrews, Woodbury, Exeter, Devon, 2002, h.430mm.

**127**
**Gourd and lid**, raku, pink, made by Tim Andrews, Woodbury, Exeter, Devon, 2002, h.250mm.

*Kindly loaned by Tim Andrews.*

**Elizabeth Raeburn**
**128**
**Winged form,** raku, terracotta, made by Elizabeth Raeburn, West Pennard, Somerset, 2002, h.318mm.

*Kindly loaned by Elizabeth Raeburn.*

**129**
**Footed vessel**, raku, white with black crackle, made by Elizabeth Raeburn, West Pennard, Somerset, 2002, h.204mm.

**130**
**Winged form**, raku, white with black speckle, made by Elizabeth Raeburn, West Pennard, Somerset, 2002, h.286mm.

# Backstamps

Impressed mark of David Leach at Dartington Hall, Devon, 1930s.

Impressed mark of David Leach at Aylesford Priory, Kent, 1954.

Impressed personal marks, intaglio and in relief, of David Leach at Lowerdown Pottery since 1956. Some of his own pots have two marks – the personal and the pottery.

Impressed mark of Lowerdown Pottery since 1956, used on the standard ranges. Apprentices and students made most of the standard, stoneware tableware, to David Leach's original design.
The L for Lowerdown and the + for the crossroads on the Haytor Road, known as Lowerdown Cross, where the pottery is situated.

Impressed mark of the Leach Pottery, St Ives, Cornwall, 1920 –. One off pots, by named potters, have the potter's personal mark and the pottery mark. The Standard range of tableware was impressed with the pottery mark.

## Anomalies

If a pot has a very small base David may not have included both marks and his choice of mark is random, so that some pots bearing only the pottery mark maybe the work of David himself.

David Leach designs all the individual pots but some were thrown by other potters and then decorated by David. These pots are impressed with both the pottery mark and David's personal mark.

In this catalogue pots have been made by David Leach himself, unless stated otherwise.

Impressed mark of David Leach and Clive Bowen. Dishes were made at Shebbear Pottery, Devon, and fired at a special event in Bideford to celebrate Devon pottery, 2001.

# Chronology

**1911** born 7th May, Tokyo. Eldest son of Bernard and Muriel Leach.

**1920** St Ives, Cornwall with family, together with Hamada.

**1925** After preparatory school in Bristol, to Dauntsey's School, Wiltshire.

**1930** Apprenticeship with his father at Leach Pottery, St Ives.

**1933** Teaching pottery at Dartington Hall School, and preparing for a future Pottery at Dartington.

**1934** Pottery Managers' Course at North Staffordshire Technical College, Stoke-on-Trent. Graduated with Honours Diploma.

**1937** Returned to Leach Pottery to develop standard ware stoneware production and train team of apprentices. Introduced oil firing and many technical improvements. With Dicon Nance as engineer, designed the Leach kick wheel with its triangular wooden frame.

**1938** Bill Marshall an apprentice at St Ives, remaining until 1977. Married Mary Elizabeth Facey, lived at Pottery Cottage, Leach Pottery, St Ives. Dartington Hall scheme shelved.

**1939** Son, John, born 21st July. Bernard Leach living at Dartington with Laurie Cookes and writing *A Potter's Book*.

**1941** Landmine devastates Pottery Cottage and damages kiln shed, 9.30 p.m. 25th January. David Leach and family move to Leach family house at Carbis Bay. War service with D.C.L.I. Bernard Leach returns to run Leach Pottery, Laurie Cookes remains in Dartington.

**1941** Second son, Jeremy, born 26th March.

**1945** December, demobilised and returns to Leach Pottery. Hearing damaged during war service. Kenneth Quick, made an apprentice.

**1946** Partnership with Bernard Leach to run Leach Pottery. Steady period of development of the Pottery. Training of students and apprentices.

**1950** Pottery classes started at Penzance School of Art for evening students. Designed and made David Leach Electric Kiln.

**1951** To Norway to help start a pottery near Sandefjord.

**1953** Invited to take over pottery department at Loughborough College of Art, for one year. Developed a range of stoneware glazes for Podmores, Stoke-on-Trent.

**1954** Started pottery for Carmelite Friars at Aylesford, Kent, built two-chambered kiln.

**1955** Colin Pearson joins the Pottery at Aylesford and subsequently takes over.

**1955** End of year, partnership with Bernard Leach at St Ives ended.

**1956** Third son, Simon, born 3rd January. March, starts own pottery at Lowerdown Cross, Bovey Tracey, Devon making slipware and tin-glaze at Lowerdown with Freda Sage and son John. Students coming and going regularly. Increasingly involved in education. Continuing as visiting lecturer at Loughborough and other colleges of art.

**1961** Two-chamber, seventy cubic foot wood and oil-fired kiln built at Lowerdown. Slipware and tin-glaze abandoned in favour of stoneware and porcelain. John Maltby and Warwick Parker Student-apprentices.

**1963** Assessor on the Harrow Studio Pottery course.

**1967** Chairman, Craftsmen Potters Association. Gold medallist at Istanbul. Devised a throwable porcelain body, later made by Podmores, Stoke-on-Trent (Potterycrafts).

**1972** Joined the Crafts Advisory Committee as member of Grants panel.

**1974** Son Jeremy working at Lowerdown.

**1975** Joined the board of Dartington Pottery Training Workshop.

**1976** 'Craft of the Potter' with B.B.C Making film on his work with Robert Fournier and John Anderson. Start of Dartington Pottery Training Workshop.

**1978** Four weeks workshop tour of six centres in U.S.A., followed by regular workshop visits abroad.

**1982** Builds small, seven cubic foot gas-fired kiln, firing in large kiln ends.

**1986** Chairman Devon Guild of Craftsmen.

**1987** Awarded Order of the British Empire (OBE).

**1989** Visits Japan for the first time in sixty-nine years.

**1996** Adviser to Skills Training Workshop for Potters, Llandeilo, Wales.

**1997** Awarded Centennial Medal of the Society of Designer Craftsmen.

**2001** 90th birthday. Son Jeremy rejoins his father at Lowerdown.

**2003** Retrospective exhibition and tour, 20th Century Ceramics, Devon Guild of Craftsmen, and book.

# Principal Exhibitions

**1949** Downing's Gallery, St Ives. Solus.

**1951** Festival of Britain, Homes and Gardens pavilion – David Leach; The Country pavilion – The Leach Pottery, St Ives, Cornwall.

**1954** Midlands Group Gallery, Nottingham. Solus.

**1962** Group exhibition, Derby Museum and Art Gallery, Derby.

**1966** Craftsmen Potters Shop and Gallery, London. Solus.

**1967** International Academy of Ceramics, Istanbul. (Gold Medal).

**1969** Craftsmen Potters Shop and Gallery, London. Group exhibitions.

**1969** Exeter University, Exeter, group exhibition.

**1971** Kettle's Yard, Cambridge, Twenty British Potters.

**1972** Craftworks, Guildford, David Leach – New Work. Solus.

**1972** 'International Ceramics', International Academy of Ceramics. Victoria and Albert Museum, London.

**1973** Copenhagen Kunstindustrimuseum, Copenhagen, Denmark. Solus.

**1973** 'Craftsman's Art' exhibition. Victoria and Albert Museum, London.

**1973, 1974, 1975** Kettle's Yard Exhibition, Cambridge.

**1973** Craftwork, Guildford. Solus.

**1974** Bluecoat Display Centre, Liverpool. Two potters.

**1974** 359 Gallery, Nottingham. Solus.

**1974** Hetjens Museum, Dusseldorf.

**1975** Casson Gallery, London, Porcelain Exhibition.

**1975** Oxford Gallery, Oxford.

**1977** Somers Gallery, Heidelberg. Solus.

**1977** Cider Press Centre, Dartington Hall, Totnes. Inaugural Exhibition. Solus.

**1978** Handwerke Galerie, Munich.

**1978** Florence Duhl Gallery, New York.

**1978** Keele University, Stoke-on-Trent.

**1978** Century Gallery, Henley-on-Thames.

**1979** British Crafts Centre, London.

**1979** American Hand Gallery, Washington DC, USA. Solus.

**1980** Paul Rice Gallery, London.

**1980** New Ashgate Gallery, Farnham, David Leach and Henry Hammond.

**1980** Craftsmen Potters Shop and Gallery, London.

**1981** Stoke-on-Trent City Museum & Art Gallery, Stoke-on-Trent, Seven Studio Potters.

**1982** New Ashgate Gallery, Farnham, David Leach and Henry Hammond.

**1982** Robert Welch Gallery, Chipping Camden. Solus.

**1982** St Paul's School, London. Solus.

**1983** New Ashgate Gallery, Farnham, David Leach and Henry Hammond.

**1983** Galerie Het Kapelhuis, Amersfoort, The Netherlands, David Leach and Walter Keeler.

**1983** Front Room Gallery, Dallas, USA. Solus.

**1983** Espace La Main, Brussels, Belgium, David Leach, John Maltby, and David Lloyd-Jones.

**1983** Katharine House Gallery, Marlborough, The Great Functional Pottery Show.

**1984** Century Galleries, Henley-on-Thames. Solus.

**1984** Chestnut Gallery, Bourton-on-the-Water. Solus.

**1984** Beaux Arts, Bath, Leach Exhibition.

**1985** Elaine Potter Gallery, San Francisco, USA, British Potters.

**1985** Galerie for Englische Keramik, Marianne Heller, Sandhausen bei Heidelberg, Germany, British Potters.

**1985** Keramik Galerie, Hanover, Germany, British Potters.

**1985** Peter Dingley Gallery, Stratford-upon-Avon, David Leach and John Leach.

**1985** Norwich Castle Museum, Norwich. Solus.

**1985** Paul Rice Gallery, London. Solus.

**1985** Takashimaya Store, Osaka, Japan, Leach Potters.

**1986** Willard Collection, Washington DC, USA, British Teapots.

**1986** New Ashgate Gallery, Farnham, Leach – Three Generations.

**1986** Galerie F15, Moss, Norway and tour, Norsk-British Keramik.

**1987** Jane Hartsook Gallery, New York, USA, David Leach and John Leach.

**1987** Craftsmen Potters Shop and Gallery, London, 'The Leach Tradition – A Creative Force'.

**1987** Stoke-on-Trent City Museum & Art Gallery, 'Take 12'. Solus.

**1987** Chestnut Gallery, Bourton-on-the-Water, The Vessel.

**1988** New Ashgate Gallery, Farnham, Group exhibition.

**1989** Galerie Het Glazen Huis, Amsterdam, The Netherlands, Contemporary English Potters.

**1989** Craftsmen Potters Association at Porticus, Porticus, Llandrindod Wells.

**1989** Chestnut Gallery, Bourton-on-the-Water, David Leach.

**1989** Craftsmen Potters Shop and Gallery, London, 'Small is Beautiful'.

**1990** Contemporary Ceramics, London, Sixty Years a Potter. Solus.

**1990** Devon Guild of Craftsmen, Bovey Tracey.

**1990** Galerie Besson, London, Domestic Ware by Artist-Potters.

**1990** Bettles Gallery, Ringwood, group exhibition.

**1991** Candover Gallery, Alresford, 101 Jugs.

**1991** Godfrey Far Eastern Art, London, 'China Clay: The Eastern Tradition in British Studio Pottery'.

**1991** The British Council, India and Malaysia, 'Colours Of The Earth – Twentieth Century British Ceramics'.

**1991** New Ashgate Gallery, Farnham, Group exhibition.

**1992** Beaux Arts, Bath, Group exhibition.

**1992** Nykvarns Gallery, Sweden, Group exhibition.

**1992** Staatliche Fachshule for Keramik, Landshut, Germany, Group exhibition.

**1992** Bluecoat Display Centre, Liverpool, 'Running In The Family'.

**1993** Galerie for Englische Keramik – Marianne Heller, Sandhausen bei Heidelberg, Germany.

**1993** Beaux Arts, Bath, Group exhibition.

**1993** Cider Press Centre, Dartington Hall, Totnes, Group exhibition.

**1993** New Ashgate Gallery, Farnham, Group exhibition.

**1993** Cider Press Centre, Dartington Hall, Totnes, 'Sixty Years of Pottery at Dartington'.

**1993** St Ives Pottery Gallery, St Ives, 'The Leach-Cardew Connection'.

**1993** Mid Cornwall Gallery, Nr. Par, 'Time for Tea'

**1994** Candover Gallery, Alresford, '10th Anniversary Exhibition'.

**1994** The Scottish Gallery, Edinburgh, Scotland, 'New Ceramics'.

**1994** Contemporary Ceramics, London. Solus.

**1994** Gallery Upstairs, Henley-in-Arden, Group exhibition.

**1994** Alpha House Gallery, Sherborne, International Fine Ceramics.

**1994** Candover Gallery, Alresford, Teapots.

**1994** Crafts Council Gallery Shop, London, Teapots.

**1994** Galerie Besson, London, The Tea and Coffee Exhibition.

**1995** Paul Rice Gallery, London, British Studio Ceramics.

**1995** On Line Gallery, Southampton, Classic Ceramics.

**1995** Galerie Besson, London. Solus.

**1995** Bettles Gallery, Ringwood. Solus.

**1996** Aberystwyth Arts Centre, Aberystwyth. Solus.

**1997** Cider Press Centre, Dartington Hall, Totnes, '20 Years On'.

**1997** Museum of Mankind, London.

**1997** Galerie Besson, London. Solus.

**1997** Gallery Upstairs, Henley in Arden, joint show.

**1997** Contemporary Applied Arts, London.

**1998** Rufford Country Park, Nottingham, 'Cool Clay'.

**1998** Marianna Heller Gallery, Sandhausen – Germany.

**1998** Bettles Gallery, Ringwood, joint show.

**1998** Scottish Gallery, Edinburgh, joint show.

**1998** Woodbury Studio Gallery, Devon, joint show.

**1998** New Ashgate Gallery, Farnham, joint show.

**1998** Galerie Besson, London. Solus.

**1999** Galerie Besson, London, joint show.

**1999** Alpha House Gallery, Sherborne, joint show.

**1999** Rufford Country Park, Nottingham, 'Collections'.

**1999** Gallery Upstairs, Henley in Arden, joint show.

**1999** Chukyo University, Japan, 'Japanese Connections'.

**1999** Bettles Gallery, Ringwood, joint show.

**1999** Candover Gallery, Arlesford, joint show.

**2000** Grimmerhaus Ceramics Museum, Denmark, joint show.

**2000** Anglo-Japanese Exhibition, Dartington Cider Press Gallery, 'Soul to Soul'.

**2001** Woodbury Studio Gallery, Devon, 90th birthday celebration.

**2002** Gallery Upstairs, Henley in Arden – The Leach Family Exhibition.

**2003** Devon Guild of Craftsmen, Bovey Tracey and tour, retrospective exhibition and book, David Leach – 20th Century Ceramics.

# Public Collections in the United Kingdom

Aberdeen Art Gallery

Aberystwyth Arts Centre

The Allen Gallery, Alton

Buckinghamshire County Museum, Aylesbury

Craft Study Centre, The Surrey Institute of Art and Design,
    University College, Farnham

University College of Art and Design, Farnham

The Ulster Museum, Belfast

Fitzwilliam Museum, Cambridge

Herbert Art Gallery and Museum, Coventry

Royal Museum of Scotland, Edinburgh

Royal Albert Memorial Museum, Exeter

Art Gallery and Museum, Glasgow

Museum and Art Gallery, Hove

Abbot Hall Art Gallery, Kendal

Lotherton Hall, Leeds

Museum and Art Gallery, Leicester

National Museums and Art Galleries, Liverpool

Crafts Council Collection, London

Victoria and Albert Museum, London

Manchester Art Gallery, Manchester

Holden Gallery, Manchester

Cleveland Craft Centre, Middlesbrough

Museum and Art Gallery, Newport

Castle Museum, Norwich

Ballantyne Collection, Castle Museum, Nottingham

Museums and Art Galleries, Paisley

City Museum and Art Gallery, Plymouth

City Museum and Art Gallery, Portsmouth

Wingfield Digby Collection, Tate, St Ives

The Potteries Museum & Art Gallery, Stoke-on-Trent

Museum and Art Gallery, Swindon

Dartington Hall Trust, High Cross House, Totnes

Royal Cornwall Museum, Truro

City Art Gallery, York

# Public Collections Overseas

Danske Kunstindustrimuseum, Copenhagen, Demark

Nihon Mingeikan, Folkcraft Museum, Japan

Setagaya Museum, Tokyo

Seibu Store, Tokyo

Hitomi Art Museum, Japan

# Articles, Books and Films

Ronald G. Cooper, *The Modern Potter; A review of current Ceramic Ware in Great Britain*, John Tiranti, London, 1947.

Barbara Hepworth, 'David Leach: The Importance of Form and Colour', review of one person exhibition, Downing's Gallery, St Ives, *St Ives Times*, August 19, 1949.

Muriel Rose, *Artist-Potters in England*, Faber and Faber, London, 1955.

Michael Casson, *Pottery in Britain Today*, Alec Tiranti, London, 1967.

Griselda Lewis, *A Collector's History of English Pottery*, Studio Vista, 1969, Barrie & Jenkins, London, 1977, Antique Collectors Club, Woodbridge, Suffolk, 1985, 1987, 1999.

George Wingfield Digby, *The Work of the Modern Potter in England*, John Murray, London, 1952.

David Leach, 'Porcelain Body', *Ceramic Review*, March/April 1970.

W. A. Ismay, 'David Leach – New Work', *Ceramic Review, July/August 1972.

Emmanuel Cooper, Eileen Lewenstein editors, editions 1-11; Emmanuel Cooper editor, 12th edition, *Potters: The Illustrated Directory of Fellows and Members of the Craft Potters Association*, Ceramic Review Publishing, London, editions 1-12, 1972-2000.

Janet Leach – 'Fifty One Years of the Leach Pottery', *Ceramic Review, April 1972.

*The Craftsman's Art*, published on the occasion of an exhibition of new work by British craftsmen at the Victoria and Albert Museum, 1973, Crafts Advisory Committee, London, 1973.

David Leach, 'Lowerdown Pottery', *Ceramic Review*, May/June, number 21, 1973.

Elizabeth Cameron and Philippa Lewis, *Potters on Pottery*, Evans Brothers Limited, London, 1976.

*Craftsman of Quality*, Crafts Advisory Committee, London, 1976, 1979, (third edition).

Michael Casson, *The Craft of the Potter: A Practical Guide to Making Pottery*, British Broadcasting Corporation, London, 1977.

W. A. Ismay, 'David Leach – Stoneware and Porcelain', *Ceramic Review*, July/August, number 46, 1977.

*David Leach*, (16mm Film), Robert Fournier & John Anderson, 1977.

Robert Fournier (editor) *David Leach – A Potter's Life – With Workshop Notes*, Robert Fournier 1977, revised 1979.

David Leach, 'Elegance and Strength', *Crafts*, May/June 1979.

An Expanding Tradition – Editorial, p.3 'David Leach New Stoneware and Porcelain' British Crafts Centre, London, March 1979; *Ceramic Review,* July/August, number 58, 1979.

*Makers*, Crafts Council, London, 1980.

Gary C. Hatcher 'A Day in the Life – Apprenticing with David Leach', *Ceramic Monthly*, June, 1980.

Peter Lane – Foreword by David Leach, *Studio Porcelain*, Pitman Publishing, London, 1980.

Gisela Scholz, 'English Potters Seminar', *Keramik* (Germany), Number 4, 1982.

Mary Regan, 'The Hard Sell', *Craft Quarterly*, Summer 1982.

Peter Dormer, *The New Ceramics Trends + Traditions*, Thames and Hudson, London, 1986, 1994.

David Leach, 'Bernard Leach a Creative Force' an appreciation of Bernard Leach on the centenary of his birth, *Ceramic Review*, November/December, number 108, 1987.

Paul Rice and Christopher Gowing, *British Studio Ceramics in the 20th Century*, Barry & Jenkins, London, 1989.

Oliver Watson, *British Studio Pottery: The Victoria and Albert Museum Collection*, Phaidon Christie's, Oxford, in association with the Victoria and Albert Museum, 1990.

Sarah Ridick, *Pioneer Studio Pottery: The Milner-White Collection*, Lund Humphries, London, in association with York City Art Gallery, 1990.

W. A. Ismay 'David Leach – Sixty Years A Potter', *Ceramic Review*, September/October, number 125, 1990.

David Leach, 'Making A Teapot', *Ceramic Review*, November/December, number 126, 1990.

David Leach and W. A. Ismay, 'Pioneer Studio Pottery', *Ceramic Review*, March/April, number 128, 1991.

Eileen Lewenstein, 'China Clay: The Eastern Tradition in British Studio Pottery', *Crafts*, September/October, 1991.

Shortform, *Crafts,* May/June 1992.

John and Margaret Cushion, *A Collector's History of British Porcelain,* Antique Collectors' Club, Woodbridge, Suffolk, 1992.

David Leach, 'A Potter's Day', *Ceramic Review,* November/December, number 138, 1992.

David Whiting, editor, *Dartington – 60 Years of Pottery 1933-1993,* Dartington Cider Press, Devon, 1993.

Peter Dormer, 'Sources of Inspiration; David Leach', *Crafts,* January/February, 1993.

Review of Beaux Arts Exhibition, *Studio Pottery,* February 1993.

Liz Hoggard, 'Art of the State', *Crafts,* September/October 1993.

Shortform, *Crafts,* July/August 1993.

David Leach, 'The 30's and Beyond' in David Whiting (ed.) *Dartington – 60 Years of Pottery, 1933-1993,* Dartington Cider Press, Devon, 1993.

Emmanuel Cooper, 'An Unassuming Talent', *Ceramic Review,* September/October, number 149, 1994.

Garth Clark, *The Potter's Art: A Complete History of Pottery in Britain,* Phaidon Press, London, 1995.

David Whiting, 'David Leach: A Vital and Contemplative Potter', *Ceramics: Art and Perception,* issue 21, 1995.

Anita Besson, 'David Leach', Galerie Besson, London, 1995.

Marion Whybrow, *The Leach Legacy: The St Ives Pottery and its Influence,* Sansom & Company, Bristol, 1996.

Anne-Carole Chamier, 'Ways of seeing', *Ceramic Review,* March/April, number 158, 1996.

David Leach, Ceramic Series, *David Leach,* Aberystwyth Arts Centre, 1996.

Gary Hatcher, 'A Conversation with David Leach', *Ceramics Monthly,* January, 1997.

Anita Besson, 'David Leach and Jessamine Kendall', Galerie Besson, London, 1997.

Tanya Harrod, *The Crafts in Britain in the 20th Century,* Yale University Press, Newhaven and London, 1999.

Emmanuel Cooper, *Ten Thousand Years of Pottery,* British Museum Press, London, 2000. Previous small editions published with title *A History of World Pottery,* 1972, 1981, 1988.

Emmanuel Cooper 'A Dynasty of Potters, The Legacy of the Leach Family', *Resurgence,* November/December, 2001.

Mary Lean and Anastasia Stepanova 'Good for a Thousand Years', *For a Change,* April/May, 2001.

Jack Doherty, *Porcelain,* A&C Black, London, 2002.

Paul Rice, *British Studio Ceramics,* The Crowood Press, Ramsbury, Wiltshire, 2002.

Kathy Niblett and Tim Andrews, 'David Leach, Potter', *Ceramic Review,* March/April, number 200, 2003.

# Assistants, Apprentices and Students
# at Lowerdown Pottery

**Notes supplied by David Leach**

**Freda Sage**. 1957-1961. First student apprentice, who became a friend of the family. Helped to set up slipware production and was a sensitive decorator of moulded dishes. Left to teach at Ipswich College of Art and set up her own Pottery. Suffered greatly from arthritis and died 2002.

**John Leach**. Eldest son 1957-1960. Now well-established potter making wood-fired stoneware, functional and individual pots at Muchelney Pottery, Somerset.

**Jeremy Leach**. Second son, 1959-1962. Intermittent student. Went to Central School of Art. Technical assistant at Camberwell School of Art, taught at various schools including Harrow and Merchant Taylors. Set up small studio near Oxford. Now potting again with David Leach since June 2001. Re-establishing himself at Lowerdown (2002).

**Ian Sprague**. 1960. An Australian student who spent a year at Lowerdown after a course with Dora Billington at the Central School of Art in London.

**John Maltby**. Student apprentice 1960-63. Trained as a sculptor at Leicester School of Art, and subsequently wanted to study with Bernard Leach. This was not possible at the time so he came to David Leach to learn the basic skills. A born independent artist. Set up workshop at Crediton, Devon.

**Warwick Parker**. 1963-66. After training at Poole Pottery as a thrower, he then studied at Poole School of Art. Worked at Lowerdown for three-and-a-half years. Started his own Pottery at Maiden Newton, Dorset in 1967.

**Buster Hogan**. 1966. A potter from Melbourne, remembered as a 'strong, large, bearded Australian'.

**Kenji Funaki**. 1967. A potter from a Japanese potting family who came for a one-year studentship.

**Gary and Daphne Hatcher**. 1970-78. Two serious long-term students from Texas. Now well established at Mineola, Texas, USA.

**Robert Tinnyant**. 1970. A young Burmese student came about 1970 and has since set up a Pottery in Kingsteignton. For many years has been a member of the Devon Guild of Craftsmen.

**Chris Barchard**. 1970. A short-term student.

**Richard Brooks**. 1970-73. A nineteen-year-old Australian apprentice who came to Lowerdown from Sydney to apprentice for three years. He re-appeared October 2001 after thirty years and is one of Australia's most established and successful potters. Now potting near Sydney.

**Mary Rich**. 1961. Came to Lowerdown for a short apprenticeship of about six months. Has a Pottery near Truro, Cornwall, where she makes hand-thrown porcelain mostly decorated with liquid bright gold and on-glaze lustres.

**Simon Leach**. Third son, 1973-75. Started apprenticeship at Lowerdown before taking up a four-year apprenticeship with Westland Helicopters in Yeovil. Returned to work with his father in 1979. Started his own Pottery in Exeter, married and re-established his pottery at Silverton near Tiverton. For the last thirteen years has been potting in Spain making raku and reduction fired tableware.

**Philip Barlow**. 1977. A short-term student from New Zealand who came to Lowerdown Pottery after working with Colin Pearson.

**Tim Andrews**. 1986-93. A student apprentice 1978-1979, came for a year before being accepted as a student at the Dartington Pottery Training Workshop for over two years. After that he set up his own workshop in Exeter and South Tawton, following which he returned to share the Lowerdown workshop with David from 1986-93 making his pots and selling them from the showroom. A happy and successful arrangement for him and David Leach. Left about 1993 to set up his home and workshop at Woodbury near Exeter.

**Elizabeth Raeburn**. 1974. Spent a brief but influential time as production student in David Leach's workshop. In 1975 she moved to Somerset establishing a pottery with Rodney Lawrence. Since 1981 she has concentrated on hand-built raku.

The following students came from the Harrow vocational course for a six-to-eight-week apprenticeship in the summer vacation between the first and second year of the Harrow course:

**Christine Ann Richards, Christine Pedley, Rod Lawrence, Merryn Geddes, Nicola Raffan, Dotty Pennicott, Peter Collingbourne, Joy Wheeler, Renton Murray, Lacky Trenchard, Sarah Walton, Victor Bryant, Sue Thorley.**

These were in the period 1966-1977, years when David Leach was external examiner at the school.

**Dr Joachim Utz**. An English Literature professor at Heidelberg University who was never a student or an apprentice in the usual sense but a very apt learner who David helped to set up his own Pottery near Weinheim in German. It was he who arranged David Leach's first exhibitions in Heidelberg.

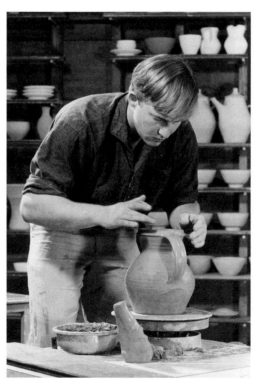

John Leach, 1963.